SCHOOL HOUSE HUMOR —AND— INSIGHT

Chuck Anderson

SCHOOL HOUSE HUMOR —AND— INSIGHT

by Chuck Sodergren

PBS

PARTNERSHIP BOOK SERVICES

Hillsboro, Kansas

Library of Congress Catalog Card Number 96-070118
ISBN 0-9645085-9-1
Cover Design: Denise Brueggeman-Siemens, Mennonite Press
Cover Illustration: Jeremy Rizza
Copy Editing: June Galle Krehbiel

The author assumes no responsibility for errors, inaccuracies, omissions or any other inconsistency herein. These writings represent the creative action of the author. The descriptions herein do not correspond to actual persons or events.

Sodergren, Chuck
School house humor and insight / Chuck Sodergren.
p. cm.
Includes bibliographical references and index.
Preassigned LCCN: 96-70118
ISBN 0-9645058-9-1

1. Education, Secondary--United States. 2. Education, Secondary--United States--Humor. 3. Junior high schools--United States. 4. Junior high schools--United States--Humor.   I. Title.

LB1623.S64 1996   373
QBI96-40301

Dedication

To my talented and dedicated teammates in the education profession.

To all of my former students and their parents.

To the members of Trinity Lutheran Church in Topeka, Kansas.

To Bernie Johnson, who has been my inspiration for over thirty years.

To my wife, Myra, and our family. I have been truly blessed.

ABOUT THE AUTHOR

Charles (Chuck) Sodergren retired from the Seaman School District, Topeka,

Kansas in May of 1995. He was the last retiree of an elite group of administrators

who formed the Seaman District when it was unified in 1965.

Chuck was born on February 16, 1934 in Topeka. His sister Barbara Apps is

two years older and recently retired from government work.

Chuck graduated from Topeka High School in 1951. He attended Washburn

University and later transferred to Bethany College, Lindsborg, Kansas where he

received his bachelors degree in Education in 1956. While at Bethany he

participated in football, basketball and track. He also participated in the world

renowned Lindsborg Messiah Chorus. Chuck received his Masters degree in

education from the University of Kansas in 1962.

After graduation, Chuck served in the Navy. He began boot camp in San

Diego and later worked as a hospital corpsman at El Toro Marine Base, California.

His educational experience began as a teacher and assistant basketball coach at

Spring Hill High School in Spring Hill, Kansas. Later, he taught at Lyman Grade

School, Topeka, Kansas. Chuck served as principal of the Grade School at Dover,

Kansas for 3 years. He then moved to the Seaman district north of Topeka where he

served as prinicipal 9 years at East Indianola Elementary school and 21 years at

Logan Jr. High.

In 1965 Chuck started the Junior Viking Sunrise Optimist basketball program.

He later served as president of the Sunrise Optimist Club, 1973. He worked in

Seaman's Outdoor Education program and is a lifetime member of Trinity Lutheran

Church, Topeka. He is a charter member of the North Topeka Historical Society.

Chuck married Myra Shoreen on November 23, 1956 in Los Angeles, California. They have four children: Janice Henry, Jane Lewis, Steve Sodergren and Janeen Horton. They have nine grandchildren.

The friends, acquaintances and loved ones of Chuck received the following notice:

On May 21, 1995, Logan Junior High School's staff will bid a fond farewell to its principal of the last twenty-one years, Chuck Sodergren. His presence is woven into the history of Logan; in many minds, Chuck Sodergren has been synonymous with Logan for over two decades. Chuck has rightfully earned widespread respect with his leadership style based on dedication, approachability and sincere concern for everyone involved in the Logan community. His retirement arouses memories of the celebrations, tragedies, twists of fate, and humorous moments we had shared. He has influenced the lives of everyone at Logan in a very personal and individual way, and he will be sorely missed at Logan. We wish him the best of luck in his new role as a retiree.

Contents

Introduction–

Slow Driver in the Fast Lane of Life

page 1

The ABC's of Middle School

page 3

CPR for Those Who Remain

in the Trenches

page 45

Introduction

Slow Driver in the Fast Lane of Life

The middle school years could definitely be considered the "fast lane of life." The physical body is growing so rapidly that the different parts have a difficult time even recognizing each other. The adolescent is on an emotional roller coaster. His curriculum needs are rapidly progressing from learning something about everything to learning everything about something. He is making decisions concerning careers, male-female relationships, and hundreds of other things that will affect his entire lifetime. Boys and girls enter middle school not much interested in each other. They experience sexual maturity like fireworks on the Fourth of July. Some would say that middle school students are the most difficult age group to work with; elementary students obey because they fear and respect authority, and you can reason with high school students, but middle school students do not fit easily into either category. Their political views and concepts of social justice will probably never again be further to the left. Adolescents are definitely in the far left lane, the fast lane, the experimental lane of life.

The middle school principal, on the other hand, has not only completed his own fast lane experiences years ago, but he has also observed thousands of others complete the journey. Every time he goes to the supermarket, he is greeted by a middle-aged adult sometimes with a bald head and beard and is asked to identify him as a kid he had in school years ago. The principal lives a much slower, more conservative, and more cautious life than he did back when he was in the fast lane himself. He can now be considered to be driving through life slowly in the far right lane.

I have written the following from my perspective as a principal, as I experienced being a slow driver in the fast lane of life. When I see a sign that says, "Slow drivers keep right," I know that the sign is referring to me.

Much of what I have recorded here as fact did not really happen. Names have been changed so as to not embarrass the innocent. Much material was cut because it would either offend some people or because it so specifically targeted educational issues that it would be boring to most.

This collection of writings is incomplete. Living our daily lives is a process of constantly editing, revising, and adding to. We should never allow "our book" to be considered complete. To do so would mean we are done living. Sir James Jeans wrote, "To travel hopefully is better than to arrive." I will continue to revise, edit, and add to my book until my final, mortal address becomes the cemetery. I hope to go to heaven because I hear that for school principals the "other place" is one eternal never-ending basketball game, complete with cheerleaders, pep clubs, and screaming parents.

My priorities, sense of humor, and appreciation of excellence are a little different than what it is for most people. For 38 years I didn't miss many days of being in the trenches of a school building and rubbing elbows with adolescent-aged kids. I can boast that I have eaten well over 6,000 school lunches (every one of them with the kids) and have enjoyed every minute of it. My wife, Myra, and I have raised four children of our own and are proud grandparents of nine. These qualifications give me a much different perspective than most other people. Will Rogers said, "There's no trick to being a humorist when you have the whole government working for you." When it comes to education related humor and insight, I have been fortunate to spend most of my life in the "fertile soil" of the school system.

I write because I enjoy writing and have thoughts that I don't want to forget. I am greatly indebted to my teammates on the Education Team. Anyone of them could have written this because they have experienced many of the same things that I have. But I will admit that I am kind of proud that I not only talked about doing it—I did it!

The ABCs of Middle School

Anecdotes, Birdwalking, and Chuckles

An anecdote is a short, entertaining story of some happening, usually personal or biographical. When a teacher gets off the subject, he or she is said to be birdwalking. We may not recall much about the content that those respected teachers have taught us, but it is amazing how much of their birdwalking we remember. Because my name is Chuck, I define a chuckle as a funny thing that happened to Chuck. I wrote the following short ABCs in my diary over a period of many years.

Open House—Tonight we held our annual Open House. Some teachers suggested holding it at some newer school or even maybe at a hotel or motel. That idea got voted down because I told them you can't have Open House in somebody else's house and that some of the teachers would demand travel pay and it wouldn't be approved. About five minutes before it was time to leave home to go to the school, I noticed that my shoes needed to be shined. While shining them, I realized that they smelled quite badly on the inside. I quickly poured a good quantity of foot powder in each shoe, put them on, and was off to Open House. The program began by having all of the parents gather in the gym so I could introduce each of the staff members. We had talked about spicing up the introductions by having each staff member run in when his or her name was called, jump up in the air, come down doing the splits like cheerleaders do, and yell, "Hi, I'm Mrs. Whatever." That idea went down by a 36-2 vote at the staff meeting. We resigned ourselves to doing it the dull way. I noticed that the crowd was really getting into it. They were howling and laughing with each introduction so much that I started to feel that maybe I had finally become what I always had wanted to be: a great public speaker. Then the awful truth became evident. Each time I made an introduction, I was stepping forward briskly and a large white cloud of foot powder was puffing up into the air. My dark blue pants were now a very light blue color up to the knees, and my shoes were almost white. A pile of white powder surrounded the podium. At least my feet didn't smell or itch.

Trying Out As An Umpire—Bert is not content to be the world's greatest math teacher. He dreams of being a major league baseball umpire. I can identify with Bert because I have always dreamed of being an auctioneer or country and western singer who specializes in yodeling. Bert currently umpires on weekends and during the summer at the high school and college level. He was notified about a week ago that a major league scout was scheduled to evaluate his performance as an umpire. He asked me to help him out by attending the game last night and yelling terrible things from the stands so he could show off how well he can handle stress and keep in control of the game by ejecting trouble makers. I thought our performance went just as we had planned it. Unfortunately, the scout agreed with the criticism that I had so mercilessly yelled at Bert. The scout said that at first he thought Bert was doing a great job and he hadn't noticed the finer details that I had so vigorously pointed out. Later he decided that I was right and that my logic had convinced him that Bert was a terrible umpire. The education profession needs great teachers like Bert anyway.

Observed Halloween—This morning we had our annual Halloween parade. We have a difficult time getting many parents to attend my talks about curriculum, but they come out in droves for the Halloween parade. I was lining up the contestants for the judging of costumes when I made a terrible mistake. A grandmother of one of the kids came to the school to observe the parade and I mistook her for a contestant in the "ugly witch" category. I held onto her arm and shoulder and led her toward the judges. Fortunately, before I got her to the judging area, I noticed that she was not a kid and muttered some story about how glad we were that she had come to visit the school and that I was only trying to get her a better place to view the judging of the costumes. She thanked me and said she had known me for years. She reminded me that I had asked her to the prom when we were both in high school. She turned me down then but thought maybe she should have gone with me because I "hadn't turned out too bad after all." (How humbling!)

The incident reminded me of an incident last year when a kid told one of our female teachers, who dressed up like a witch, that she looked like his mom. I told him that wasn't a very nice thing to say about his mom. He said that he didn't mean it as it sounded; his mom dressed up like a witch for Halloween and the costume looked like the teacher's. It also reminded me of the time last year when I went shopping with Myra. She was looking at some dresses in the ladies section and I was waiting for her across the aisle in the men's department. I was standing there, real still, holding some packages, when a lady backed up to me and touched me. I moved a little and the lady jumped back startled and said loudly, " I thought you were a statue." I told Myra about the incident and she said that the lady must be stupid. Why would they make a mannequin that looked like me? They make mannequins young and handsome. Whenever I see someone standing or sitting very still I am tempted to say, "Oh, I thought you were a statue."

The Football Team and the Gas Gauge — Yesterday our middle school football team was returning on a bus after a game in Junction City, which is about 60 miles from our school. They had about 10 miles to go and the gas gauge was on "empty." Our head coach was driving the bus. He told one of his players, known for his keen wit, to kneel down next to him and if the bus started to sputter from lack of gas, he should break the glass over the gauge and pull the needle up with his finger and hold it up to keep the bus going. It was tense for a while, but when the bus rolled in safely in front of the school, the young man relaxed, stood up, and humbly acknowledged thanks from the entire team. We are expecting the "hero" to brag about the incident for the rest of the year. We all got a good laugh when the coach told us about it, very privately.

Caught Red-Handed — A week ago today, I decided to bring new meaning to the saying, "caught red-handed." Our staff reported to me that they had observed several boys go into the school restroom and then emerge smelling like they had been smoking. There was always smoke in the air after they were in the restroom, but we couldn't seem to catch them in the act of smoking. I confronted them and searched them but found no cigarettes. We discovered that they had been hiding some cigarettes up in the ceiling tile and guessed that they had been reaching them by standing on the heat radiator. I planned to "catch them red-handed" by placing a jar cap filled with red colored water (using red dye that was left over from coloring Easter eggs) up in the ceiling next to the cigarettes, so that the boys would get their hands red when they reached up to get the cigarettes. We watched them go into the restroom for several days but saw no red hands. I have to admit it was getting to be a little fun, like going fishing and waiting for my bobber to move. Yesterday I thought that I had better check the trap to see if the lid with the red dye was still there. I stood up on the radiator, carefully moved a piece of ceiling tile over a few inches, and reached in. The red dye was still there, and I knocked it over. The red water stained the ceiling tile and dripped all over my white shirt. I was caught "red-faced." We never did catch the boys doing anything wrong.

I've been caught before. Once I set six mouse traps in the garage, and then forgot about them. I went out there at night, stepped on them, and thought someone was shooting at me. And the time I searched kids for a stink bomb, and discovered later that the bad smell was caused by material put in a drain by the custodian to open up a clog. The smell brought back pleasant memories of preparing lutfisk for smorgasbords at church. One of the kids that I searched said, "I want my attorney, Jesus Christ!" My vice-principal, Curt, overheard this and asked me, "What was the name of that kid's lawyer?" The next day I got a letter with the return address of a law firm, and thought I was in trouble. Much to my relief, the lawyer was only promoting an Optimist Club oratory contest.

Eternal Turn Indicator—A few years ago, our church was given an "Eternal Flame Set." It hangs up in front of our church and the candle in it must be changed regularly. Last Sunday I noticed that it had gone out. I wondered, "What will happen now? Has the eternal flame on John Kennedy's grave ever gone out? What would happen if it did?" My son-in-law Bob said that I have a tendency to have an "Eternal Turn Indicator" on my car and that I should have one on my grave. I forget to turn it off once in a while. My family likes to remind me of the time that they thought it would be funny to let me drive all the way across Wyoming with my left-turn indicator blinking.

The K-9 Teacher—We needed to hire another teacher because we had more kids show up at school this year than we had expected. We were looking over one applicant's credentials and my assistant principal commented, "She's K-9" (meaning of course that she is certified to teach grades kindergarten though nine). Thinking it would be funny, I said, "Why would we want to hire a dog?" When she arrived for the interview, we could hardly keep from laughing out loud. She really did resemble a dog—and we hired her.

Know-A-Guys—We have all heard of guys who know a guy who knows a guy who is famous for some reason. I found out today that I am only three "know-a-guys" away from most of the movie stars in Hollywood. My son-in-law Curt knows a guy in Minnesota whose daughter married a movie star's brother. Curt saw the wedding picture and testified that there were a lot of movie stars at the wedding. This got me to thinking how small a world this is and how we are all sort of connected in some way to each other. Our high school football coach was a boyhood buddy of the baseball star Mickey Mantle. I also found out that a lady who I have been going to church with for years, is a cousin of a famous sports announcer's dad. He knows all kinds of big shots. Jacob Bronowski said, "Sooner or later, every one of us breathes an atom that has been breathed before by anyone you can think of who has lived before us—Michelangelo or George Washington or Moses." I was feeling very philosophical tonight and was telling my wife that when I sit on the toilet seat I experience the tremendously satisfying feeling of being somehow connected by the pipes that lead from the bathroom to all of mankind and that I have something in common with everyone who has ever lived. She reminded me that the pipes running from our bathroom lead only to our backyard septic tank and that it was true that I have much in common with a septic tank.

Recycling—Two of the most elegant and highly respected ladies at our church have been sending the same birthday card back and forth to each other for years. Dorothy Peterson's birthday is on November 19th, and Dorothy Anderson's birthday falls on September 21st. They have one birthday card that says, "HAPPY BIRTHDAY TO DOROTHY," and is signed, "from Dorothy."

One of my administrator friends told me how he pulled off a similar "best wishes recycling deal." It was Bosses Day, so his staff gave him a cute coffee mug filled with candy and the words "When the boss is happy, everybody is happy" inscribed on it. He was really impressed that his staff had thought of him and had gone to all of the trouble to get him a present. He thanked them sincerely. He decided to take the gift over to the central office and give it to the superintendent. Everyone came out ahead on a deal like that. His staff got the satisfaction of showing him appreciation. My administrator friend was a double winner, and his boss felt good too.

A teacher who I have worked with for over 30 years, Ole Johnson (the school district clerk had his personnel folder filed with the Y's because that is the way he pronounces his last name) told me about a triple play recycle deal that really takes it all. Ole's elderly aunt died so he took off work to attend her funeral. After the services he was urged to take some of the beautiful flowers home. On the way home he remembered that it was his wife Ruth's birthday so he gave her the flowers. She was thrilled that he had remembered and gone out of his way to buy flowers. About that time they received word that they had just been made grandparents again. Ruth suggested that they should take some flowers to the new parents and grandchild and suggested, a little apologetically, that they might as well give them the flowers that Ole had given her. She said that she really appreciated the thoughts conveyed by Ole's gift of flowers to her and hoped that Ole didn't take offense to the suggestion. Ole smiled and said that he understood and agreed to the arrangement.

That reminds me of the story that my aunt Esther told about the annual Christmas gift exchanges that she had with her brother Otto. Uncle Otto lived in Kansas City. He had always been kind of a mystery man to us. Every Christmas he had traveled the 75 miles to Topeka by bus to visit with Esther for a few days. One year we were surprised to learn that he had been married for over 25 years to a really great lady and, for some unexplained reason, had kept it a secret from all of us, including his own dear sister. Every Christmas, for over ten years, Esther had given the same shirt to Otto. Every year, when Otto went back to Kansas City, he didn't take the shirt, and Esther wrapped it up and gave it to him again the next Christmas. Finally, one Christmas, Otto laughingly said, "I don't like this shirt, and I never have."

Every year it works out that Memorial Day comes just a few days after our school graduation ceremony. We always have lots of flowers left over from the ceremony. I hate to see them go to waste and am always tempted to put them to good use by decorating my parents' graves with them. I've never done it because somebody would probably find out and the media would have a field day at my expense.

As well as recycling "best wishes," I have also been involved in passing on some rather negative (or we see them as humorous) messages. Today someone put an unopened tube of hemorrhoid jelly in my mailbox. It had an expiration date on the label of ten years ago. The unwritten message had to be either that I AM a pain in the rear-end, or that I HAVE a pain there that I make very obvious. It started making the rounds in other teachers' mailboxes, but for some reason, it always ended up back in my box. One teacher said that maybe it was worth some money as a rare item. I finally wrapped it up and sent it to our high school principal.

I have been flooded (pardon the pun) with material which has been sent to me from companies, selling programs that cure bed wetting and hearing aids. My buddies sent my name in to these outfits requesting information. I'll have to admit that I've requested my share of information for them so I guess we're even.

I'll Hit You Again—The largest and toughest boy in the school (6'6" tall and weighing 250 pounds), was walking down the hall between classes. He suddenly experienced a cramp in his leg so bad that he found it necessary to lie down on the floor. I happened to see him and went over to check out what the problem was. While he was explaining his problem to me a very large crowd gathered. Taking advantage of the situation, I said very loudly, "One more word out of you and I'll hit you again." It never hurts to do whatever one can to bolster respect.

Be Nice To All Kids, All of the Time—I would rather take a beating than go to the dentist. It all started back in 1946 when I made my first "solo" trip. The dentist's office was on the tenth floor. I remember him as a Frankenstein-type guy. A big midwestern thunderstorm hit Topeka about the same time that I sat down in the dentist's chair. The dentist (who in my memory, I shall always refer to as "Frank") watched the lightning while he drilled my teeth. He just mutilated my mouth. I can still hear the loud sound of that primitive drill!

Years later, when I was in the Navy, I went to get my teeth worked on at the El Toro Marine base. Two Navy dentists took turns working on me. They were joking around and having a great time just as if I weren't even there. They pried my mouth wide open, and while my saliva dripped all over, they took a ten minute break. I could hear them in the next room laughing and betting on a football game. In my condition, I couldn't make a sound. All of this led me to hate going to the dentist, so I didn't for years.

Word around town was that a new dentist, who was really great, had just begun his practice. Myra convinced me to let her get me an appointment with him. I hoped that at last, I would be lucky enough to meet a nice dentist who wouldn't hurt me. I had given up going solo long ago, so Myra and I went into the dentist's office together. He got me strapped in the chair and was ready to begin working on me when he said, "Mr. Sodergren, do you remember me?" I looked into his face for a few seconds and sure enough, I recognized him as a kid whom I had suspended from school when he was in the seventh grade. I uttered some noise and started stuttering. He reassured me that he had no hard feelings toward me and told me to relax. He did a great job with no pain and very little discomfort.

From now on, I am going to be nice to all kids all of the time. You never know, any one of them could end up being my dentist!

When I was a senior in college, I reluctantly approached a representative of a large company that sold supplies to schools and asked him to buy a ten dollar ad in the college football program. He rudely refused, and explained in a sarcastic manner that those people who buy school supplies don't read college football programs. Years later I remembered this experience when I was no longer a college kid but a school principal. For over twenty-five years I made it a point never to buy supplies from that particular company. I finally mellowed on the topic, but I know for sure that by refusing to spend ten dollars that company lost over a hundred thousand dollars' worth of business. College kids don't remain college kids forever. Businessmen had better be nice to all kids all of the time! One of them could end up being a potential customer!

The Bad Weather Trip To School—The weather was terrible today! It snowed all night, and then about an inch of frozen rain fell on top of the snow. In the good old days the weather man would have described the size of hail by comparing it to golf balls, tennis balls, or baseballs. On other occasions he would compare it to the sizes of various kinds of fruits. I have noticed that recently he has started to compare the size of hail to pocket change, like nickels, dimes, and quarters. I told Ole that this trend goes to show how the values of our society have changed. He thinks I have made too much of it.

The superintendent called off school, but that never stops Ole and me from going to school anyway. It just makes getting there a challenge. After all of these years, we are both like homing pigeons or old fire horses. I was relieved when Ole called and asked if I wanted him to come by and pick me up. My car is not good on the ice. I told Myra how great a guy Ole was, thinking of me on such a slick day and always willing to help. I can always count on my good friend, Ole. On this particular morning, we got to school without incident. Much to my surprise, I overheard Ole telling the custodian that he got caught without sand bags in his truck (to give the truck weight to help it operate better in the snow) so he thought of me. He "thought it would be easier to use Chuck's 250 pounds than to go buy sand bags." So much for thoughtfulness.

     Christmas Pageants—All of the recent court rulings on the separation of church and state have made it illegal to have a nativity scene or Christmas pageant at school featuring the story of Christ's birth. It might be interesting to go ahead and do it and get sent to prison. All of the hardened criminals would ask me, "What ya in for?" and I would answer with some martyr type of statement. On the other hand, my own painful memories of being relegated to being the next-to-the-top branch on the right side of the Christmas tree by just standing there and holding a green piece of paper make me happy that some poor modern kid will not need to suffer such indignity. I always felt that the rich kids, school board members' kids, and doctors' and lawyers' kids were selected to play the parts of Mary, Joseph, angels, and wise men. Us poor kids were sheep, cows, and in my case, a branch of the Christmas tree.

     The Substitute Counselor—Our regular counselor had to miss work for a period of time while on maternity leave. A teacher who worked in the after-school program was helping us carry out some of the functions usually taken care of by the counselor. I jokingly told him that I would give him a short course on being a counselor. I told him that all he needed to do was:

(1) Ask the person to tell what happened or why he wanted to see you. Say, "Tell me all about it."

(2) Keep eye contact, and regularly nod and say, "Ah-ha."

(3) Ask him to tell you how he feels about that or how that made him feel.

(4) Ask him to tell you what he would do differently if he did it again.

     When our regular counselor heard about my feeble attempt at humor, she came up with the following short course on how to be a principal:

    (1) Be born ugly.

    (2) Talk about one thing so long that everyone will agree to anything just to get away.

    (3) Don't hear well, and even if you do hear something, act like you don't.

    (4) Become a master at double-talk and "looking into it."

     We declared a truce, and I said that I would look into it. If she said anything more, I didn't hear what it was.

Shopping Trips—We went to the mall tonight. On the way there, I said to my little granddaughter, "Look in that mirror and see if the ugly old man that I saw in there the last time I looked, is still in there." She looked in the car mirror and said, "No Grandpa, only a pretty young girl is in there."

I let Myra and the grandkids off at the door because the weather was terrible. As I was pulling away to find a parking place, Myra commented, "Don't forget where you park." I was offended, and said sarcastically, "Have I ever forgotten where I park?" She replied, "Disneyland 1974." She was right so I said no more.

I always go out of my way to meet one of those hired opinion takers that work at the mall. I love to find someone who will listen to me and cares what I think. Big let down. She was looking for someone younger to interview. Myra thinks that they don't pick me to interview because they remember some of the things I said once when I was trying to be funny.

One day when I was sitting on a bench holding my baby grandson, some old ladies came up and said, "Hi there, cutey, you're so sweet I would like to take you home with me." I was shocked until I realized that they were referring to my grandson.

I've always enjoyed walking in stores and just looking around. Myra and I do this often on vacations and also on normal weekends around the Topeka area. If we allowed ourselves to buy something every time, these outings could get very expensive. To prevent this from happening, and also to give the impression that we are not just taking up space that is needed for real customers, I have developed a list of three things to look for that I am sure we will never find. This way we will save money by never feeling obligated to buy something. The store unfortunately just doesn't have what we are looking for.

I am looking for (1) a brass monkey equipped with the necessary accessories to allow me to know how cold it is outside, (2) a coffee mug with the name "Myra" on it, and (3) a photograph, that I had seen years ago, with a school burning in the background, a football game proceeding in the foreground, and a large crowd that is watching the football game with great interest and no concern whatsoever about the burning school. I would hang the picture in my office and label it "Priorities." When a clerk comes up to us and says, "Can I help you find something?", I tell her exactly what three things we are looking for. We can always count on that clerk not bothering us again.

It would ruin all of our fun if we ever found these three things. We've had a few close calls. One store in Sacramento had brass monkeys but, fortunately, they were very small and not properly equipped.

It is lots of fun to walk through department stores and try out all of the free samples of perfume and cologne. We spray them on each other and smell for hours. We got a little scared once when I accidently sprayed some in my eye but the damage was only temporary. Too may adults are too "cool" to do this type of thing. "Cool" people don't have much fun. They think they are too mature to do spur of the moment acts. They don't know what they are missing!

Multi-Cultural Program at its Worst—The first thing I did when I arrived at school early one morning was to run off some suspicious looking outsiders who were hanging around in the commons area. I could tell right away, by just looking at them, that they were trouble makers. They looked, spoke, and acted weird. They were even different races than kids in our school. They talked back to me and kept trying to make me change my mind about making them leave. I got them out the front door and was about to call school security when our social studies teacher came to my office and told me that he was expecting a group of foreign exchange students to arrive any time. He had arranged for them to spend the day talking to his classes about their various cultures. Our staff had voted to make "multi-cultural awareness" one of our major goals for the year. We were teaching kids not to judge people negatively because they look different than themselves and have different cultural traditions and folkways. I thought, "My gosh, I kicked them out!" I hurried outside and tried to undo any damage I had done. Our guests were more understanding than I would have been and agreed not to tell the staff and kids about my mistake. They laughed about it—or were they laughing at me? Either way, I had it coming. I decided that they are all very smart people because they can speak more than one language and I can't.

The Bank Field Trip—Our eighth grade Economics class took a tour of the local bank. Because of the makeup of the class and the possible problems that could happen if some of these kids got close to money, I thought I better go along to beef up supervision. The kids behaved great and everything went well except that I got a terrible feeling when I found out that everything a person says when sitting in his car while waiting at the drive-up window echoes loudly all over the working section of the bank. I got embarrassed when I remembered some of the "cute" things that I usually say like: (1)What if my hand got cut off in that machine and it went flying into the bank-ha ha, (2)Boy I wish they would hurry up, (3)Shall I tell them we have kids at home? Maybe they would give us some free bubble gum, and (4) Gosh, that lady is ugly!

And I really get embarrassed when I remember that I had most of those workers in school at one time or another and they know me.

The Watergun—I took a watergun away from a kid last week. It was a very realistic looking gun. I thought it would be fun to take it home to let the grandkids play with it. Myra met me at school because we had planned go out to eat together after work. I asked her to put the watergun in her purse so I wouldn't forget it. We stopped at K-Mart to buy some things and the clerk got a real scare when Myra opened her purse to get her check book and the realistic looking gun fell out. We explained the situation before the police could be called. Thank goodness we didn't try to board an airplane.

Nerds and Arbor Day—The Student Council sponsored "Spirit Week." I suggested that one of the special days could be "Nerd Day" and that all of the kids could come to school dressed like a Nerd. The daily announcements read, "If you want to know what a Nerd looks like, see Mr. Sodergren."

The Chess Club is planning to have an Arbor Day poster contest next Spring. They argued about whether spelling should count off or if they should judge the posters only on their message and art work. This battle will rage on for the next several months and I will probably have to step in and settle it.

A Trip To The Doctor—I went to the doctor today. I never know whether or not I should ask Myra to go with me. If I do, I feel kind of like a little kid having to have my "momma" go in with me, but if I don't, I'm never sure what the doctor told me. I also am never sure if I should urinate before I go. It would be bad to get in there with the doctor poking all over me and have to go to the bathroom. It might be worse if I can't fill the specimen bottle. I'm sure of one thing though; I always wear my best underwear—no holes.

Something always happens when I go to the doctor's office that embarrasses me. This time it was when the pretty young nurse had me take a chest x-ray. I took my shirt off and she stood me up facing the wall with my chin raised and my arms straight. Then she said real nice "take a deep breath and hold it." I took a deep breath, my fat stomach went in, and my pants fell down to my feet. The nurse was nice and acted like she didn't even notice it.

Boys Arm Wrestling With Girls—I was telling Myra this morning that I had made a new rule at school forbidding any boy from arm wrestling with a girl. I went on to say that a boy has nothing to gain. If he wins, people say, "So what, you should beat a girl," and if he loses he will never live down the disgrace. I told her about a high school friend who had lost in an arm wrestling contest to a girl and people still referred to him forty years later as "The guy that a girl beat in arm wrestling." Myra said that she agreed with me and told about a teacher that she had in junior high school who wore the same necktie every day all year. Years later kids could never remember his name but referred to him as the "Old man who always wore the same necktie." It is great that I have a wife who is so perceptive, but I wish that she would have just come right out and told me that I needed to change my tie because I had worn the same one all year.

Teacher Habits—I saw a T-shirt today that had the following written on it: "It'll be a great day when the schools will get all the money they need and the Air Force will have to hold a bake sale to buy a bomber." Wow! That is terrific. I probably wouldn't have noticed the writing on the shirt if I hadn't developed the habit of checking all writing on T-shirts for profanity. I even catch myself "supervising the crowd" when the family goes to major league baseball games. During intermission at any and all programs that I go to, even 1,000 miles from home in the summer time, I find the best place to see the crowd and before I know it I'm "supervising." Our staff went as a group to a fancy place to eat on the last day of school last year, but we didn't succeed in generating much togetherness because each and every one of us had been conditioned to sit facing the crowd and nobody would sit on the other side of the table.

I'm not the only one who brings school teacher habits home with me. My daughter just started teaching first grade this year and is already responding to what I say with "Thank you for sharing that with us, Dad." She asked a friend who wasn't talking much at a party, "Do you have something you would like to share with the group?" We both catch ourselves calling the house the "building." We went out to eat together and I was discussing the fact that waitresses get tips and we don't get them in our jobs. She agreed that we don't get monetary tips but said that she has sure gotten plenty of the advice type of "tips" since she started teaching.

Our Remodeling Project—Myra and I decided to do some remodeling of the interior of our house. It had been a long time since we had done this. Some of the marks which were made by our kids seeing how high they could jump when they were in middle school were still on the ceilings. Now they have kids of their own doing the same thing. When we work together on a project, I am anxious to get to the real manly and important stuff, like sawing and hammering, and she holds up progress by insisting on doing irrelevant trivia like measuring, matching colors, and planning. I think that stuff is sissy-like and wimpish, but I have learned to keep my mouth shut because she is inevitably right, and I hate to have to admit it later.

One of our major goals was to remodel our own bedroom, so we had to sleep in different rooms for a few nights. Some of the really great discoveries of life are made by accident and we really hit the jackpot this time! By sleeping in different rooms and in beds that were not very comfortable we got the sensation of being on vacation. We had the feeling of being on vacation without driving a mile, making room reservations, or paying one penny. The longer and more exotic the vacation that you don't take, the more money that you save. We only saved about 300 dollars this year because we didn't go to Branson, Missouri. Next year we'll be smarter and save more by not going to Sweden or maybe Hawaii. Now all we have to do is market the idea and we will be rich.

Picking a Pope and Picking a Superintendent—Our superintendent retires at the end of this year. The school board is busy interviewing possible replacements. All of this has been done in an atmosphere of secrecy and everyone in the local education community is anxious to find out who they pick. I suggested that maybe they could communicate how the process is going like the College of Cardinals of the Roman Catholic Church does when they pick a new Pope. We could all sit around outside of the building and wait to see what color of smoke comes out of the chimney. The idea was not well received.

Mixed Marriage—Myra and I get along great, considering the fact that we have a mixed marriage—she likes decaffeinated coffee and I prefer regular. We also have different abilities. She puts pop into the refrigerator, and I take it out and drink it. Once at school I was about to complain that it seems like I'm the only one who knows how to make coffee when my secretary commented that it seemed to her that she must be the only one who knows how to put paper into the copy machine.

Thirteen Supervision Techniques—Lunchroom supervision and putting on deodorant have one thing in common; you only do it once a day but how well it gets done determines how well the rest of the day goes. I have identified the following thirteen supervision techniques:

(1) "Scare Crow." Just be physically present, no need to act or even move. Your mere presence will scare away any potential trouble. Place a lifesized cardboard cutout of you in the hallway at night after you go home.

(2) "Put up with no foolishness." This is a stance more than a technique. Arms must be crossed across the chest—no smile or movement—legs slightly apart.

(3) "Harvey Wall Hanger." Observers wonder if the supervisor is holding up the wall behind him or vise versa.

(4) "Swedish Step-Pivot." This technique is designed for 360 degree supervision. The left foot stays permanently in one spot; right leg

steps once and then pivots on left foot. Especially good on playgrounds, lunchroom, and in hallways. (Non-Swedes may prefer to use opposite feet.)

(5)   "Intermittent Shot Gun Blast." On a regular schedule do something, not aimed at anyone in particular, to let your presence be known to scare off potential trouble (like a shot gun blast scares off birds in a garden or orchard).

(6)   "Lifeguard." Situate yourself high up or otherwise in a position to observe the entire scene to be supervised and intermittently sweep the area with your eyes and then spot check, with special attention to "deep water areas" (likely problem spaces).

(7)   "Fisherman." Patiently watch for the need to act, and respond "when the bobber moves."

(8)   "Secret Service." At assemblies and athletic contests, dress in a dark blue suit and conservative necktie and concentrate on surveying the crowd and totally disregard the purpose for the gathering.

(9)   "Dark Alley Detective." Sneak, hide, and spy technique use to catch criminals in the act.

(10)   "Traffic Cop." Stand where you can't be seen and catch speeders (students going beyond allowed limits).

(11)   "Just Happen To Need To Wash My Hands." Used to check restrooms without admitting that you suspect something. Caution: hands get chapped if used extensively.

(12)   "Columbo." Purposely pose incompetence in order to cause persons to loosen up their defenses and allow the supervisor or investigator to give the appearance of just "slopping onto something."

(13)   "Policeman On Beat." Keep moving to different areas to "check them out." Develop a cocky, slow "I'm in control here" swagger or strut.

Suggestions From Staff and Students—I put a "suggestion box" out on the office counter and announced over the public address system that staff and students were encouraged to write down their ideas and put them in the box. I wanted them to be free to express themselves without fear, so I told them not to put their name on the paper. A representative sample of suggestions follow: All are direct quotes.

(1)   The school should get a 900 telephone number. It would cut down on complaint calls and make money.

(2)   We should buy a convertible school bus. It would be "cool," man.

(3)   To be considered a great leader (like Abe Lincoln, Martin Luther King, George Washington, John Kennedy, or FDR) one needs to either have a war or get killed. We should make sure these happen to our principal.

(4)   Our school should have our own cemetery. Instead of getting pay
      raises as fringe benefits, staff members should get to be buried free
      along the edge of the football field. Upright tomb stones could
      double as yard markers. We would be ready for a game whenever we
      want one without having to put yard markers out. (We voted this one
      down because we wanted a pay raise and there was no plan that
      clearly defined who would get to be buried at the 50 yard line.)

(5)   We should rent our pep club out to visiting teams. We could make
      money and save them the trouble of transporting their pep club to our
      school. If the "Rent a Pep Club" idea spread to other schools, we
      could work out some kind of even trade and no money would need to
      exchange hands. (One teacher said, "To rent is stupid when you can
      own something. That's why I got married." The comment caused
      quite a stir!)

(6)   Change the name of the school office complex to "Customer Service Center."

(7)   We need more emphasis on do's than don'ts in the school.

(8)   Start a "Past Homemakers of America" chapter in the old folks home
      to go with our Future Homemakers of America (FHA) chapter. Or if
      that doesn't work, get some present homemakers and call them " FHA
      alums."

(9)   When the school gets a new bell system ask if you can have the old
      one to install in your house so you will know when it is time to eat on
      weekends and during the summer.

(10) A girl who is a cheerleader one year but isn't elected the next year
      could be a "cheerleader emeritus."

(11) Make it against the law to have artificial turf on football fields. If
      God had wanted football played on astroturf, she would not have
      made regular good old American dirt fields. Artificial turf is a
      communist plot.

(12) Video tape a lesson at regular speed. Play it back real slooow for slow
      kids; regular speed for regular kids; and fast for fast kids. Someone
      in Washington, D.C. or New York could do this for all of the kids in
      the nation. We could save money because we won't need teachers —
      only some volunteer moms to come to the school to run the VCRs.

(13) I don't like any of your stupid elective courses. Get some that would
      be fun and cool, man.

(14) Quit changing the names of Special Education classes. A rose by any
      other name smells the same. I just want to know what class I'm
      teaching. Quit confusing me!

(15) Celebrate Arbor Day by having each kid bring a branch from a tree at
      home and graft all of the branches together to make a community tree

on a common stump. It would have great symbolism!

(16) We could run the academic program of the school like we run intramurals—everyone plays and everyone wins. Or is life like that? In tee-ball, if the batter misses three pitched balls, he gets to put the ball on a tee and hit it. He is guaranteed a hit. Is life like that? NO. Let's get back to what American schools should be about—FAILING KIDS!

(17) To teach creative thinking and writing skills, give every student in the English class a plastic cup (like you get pop in at ball games) and a tennis ball. Ask him to invent a game using these—either as an individual or with other students. Everyone involved must write the rules to the game—how to score, etc. and read it to the class.

(18) The middle school library could save money by sharing the daily newspaper with the high school. We would get the same news only one day late. What's the hurry anyway? We could tape record the television and radio news and play it back the next day to keep it consistent with the day-late newspaper news. We have lots of high tech equipment so why not use it? And on the subject of sharing— people who have to share their birthday with someone else in their family should have their birthday changed to a different day.

(19) Make distinguished people in the middle school "Fellows"— Give them an "Honorary Middle School Doctorate"— or create a "Chair" in their name. We could have retired staff be "Emeritus" rather than retired. Some of our staff could be "adjunct" professors (stay at home and teach over the telephone).

(20) You keep talking about promoting "respect." Require teachers to salute the principal, kids to salute teachers, and everybody to salute the cooks and janitors. My brother said that they have to do that in the army. It would be easy. Just make it a policy and put it in the handbook.

(21) School bus drivers are expected to be friendly so they wave at patrons as they meet them while driving down the road. This could be a safety hazard. We should get automatic arm wavers on all buses or hire someone to do it.

(22) The school should sell homing pigeons. They would fly back to the school and we would never have to replenish our inventory. We could sell the same one over and over.

(23) Quit calling Northern Hills our sister school. Sister is sexist. We should call it our sibling school.

(24) The middle school staff needs to have inservice speakers on the following so they can relate to students better: (A) Motorcycles (B)

Athletic Shoes (C) Music Groups.

(25) We need to buy a camera to use to decide who wins "photo finish" races in track meets. If we can't afford to buy a camera, hire an artist to draw a picture of it, or have the art class do it.

(26) Retire and create your own line of clothing. You could get rich! Those clothes you wear are bound to get back into fashion sooner or later.

(27) I don't mind doing team teaching but I want to do it by myself.

(28) If a kid smells in class, don't say anything to him about it. Just put a stick-up deodorant unit on the bottom of his desk and he'll get the idea.

(29) Some of us girls don't have any clubs to belong to. We should form a "United Girls and Ladies Youth club" or UGLY club for us. We could meet at 7 tonight.

(30) If the principal is the real principal, is the vice principal only an imitation?

(31) Get our old roof back. That expensive new one leaks.

(32) Give out the yearbooks on the first day of school so we can enjoy them all year.

(33) I see that the city is looking for a new director at the zoo. You should apply because you have had experience running a zoo (middle school).

(34) If you think CD-ROM is a rock group, you've got a lot of technology left to learn.

(35) Make people bring in their old tooth that was pulled to prove that they went to the dentist.

(36) Kids are calmer first thing in the morning than they are at noon. Our lunch supervision would be much easier if we would have lunch as soon as the kids get here in the morning.

(37) The superintendent of schools should sponsor a food drive for the needy at Christmas time. It could be called the Soup for the Supt. program.

(38) Some of the kids that we have in school today will spend much of their adult life in prison. We should ask the warden of our state prison what we should be teaching kids to make them more successful prisoners. Preparing kids for prison should be one of our purposes.

(39) Put a label on kids when they leave school, "inspected by Mr. Sodergren," like they do on clothes when you buy them (inspected by Stella).

(40) We should hire an exorcist to work on bad kids. We could trick those who haven't been baptized into being baptized by telling them we are

going swimming and dunking them when they aren't looking or have them go for a walk past a revival tent and snatch them in.

(41) Just for fun we should put a piece of plywood over the hoop that the cheerleaders cover with paper to have the football team run through at the beginning of games. Boy, that would be funny!

(42) The Student Council should buy a "school dog." Each of the kids in the school could get to take the dog home one night a year. It could spend days in the school, be a friend to kids who need one, and clean up the lunchroom floor. Or maybe a "school cat."

(43) Don't have chili suppers on the same day as basketball games. When a big crowd gets in a gym on a cold winter night in Kansas after five consecutive nights of chili suppers, look out!

(44) Have a "Hall of Fame" and a "Hall of Shame" for past students.

(45) Don't put radiator "stop leak" in the coffee pot again no matter how bad it leaks. Last time everyone got sick.

(46) The principal would relate to the kids better if he would untie his shoe laces and wear a black shirt.

(47) Use the school volleyball nets as supports for peas to grow on in your garden this summer. It's too hot to play volleyball in the summer anyway.

(48) Have nothing but one subject all day and keep having it all day every day until all of that content has been mastered before going on to a different subject. End the year with six weeks of physical education or recess. I suggested this the last place that I worked and they tried it. I got fired. They weren't very open minded.

(49) Have the shop make some "Earthquake basketball goals." We could sell them and make lots of money. They would be made so they would swing back and forth so a person can practice hitting a moving basket. Then, if the score is tied and our team has the ball with just seconds on the clock and an earthquake hits, we would be ready for it. Or—the goal could be held up by balloons so if an earthquake hits, it would just hang there without moving.

(50) Use the "Enemies paper grading system." The kids would grade each other's papers but we would make sure that they don't cheat by having kids grade their enemy's paper.

(51) Why don't you retire and work at a roller skating rink or selling novelty flashlights, swords, and programs at the circus? Then you could get all of your friends (the only one you have—Ole Johnson) in free to celebrate each other's birthdays.

(52) To punish kids, cancel their birthday.

(53) Schedule all of the worst driver's education students to drive on the

driving range at the same time. Set up bleachers, sell tickets, and take bets on which ones survive.

(54) Don't allow anyone to be sick unless they have a good reason.

(55) Let staff members use old worn out classroom maps and phonics charts (the kind that pull down) for shades at home. Or they could be used as wallpaper in garages to settle arguments about geography or phonics when men gather there.

(56) Baseline data on student achievement should be their own parents' achievement level when they were that age. If we can get kids above that, we succeed.

(57) When true-false tests are returned to students after they have been graded, make them change all of those marked wrong to the correct answer. It would be easy to change true to false and vice-versa. We could have 100% mastery every time with this second chance method.

(58) You waste lots of time when you run off track meets. A faster way to do it would be to have all of the participants in all running events line up at the starting line at the same time. Then shoot the starting gun and have timers and pickers at the end of 100 meters, 200 meters, 400 meters, 800 meters, 1600 meters. Or you could run all at the same time with the same finish line but have different starting lines for each race. It would be like a three ring circus, or even better! And in the shot, discus, and javelin make it one-on-one match play with the winners moving on tournament style. The first guy would throw, stand where he threw from, and his opponent would throw back toward him from where his shot, discus, or javelin lit. Last person standing wins. And run the long jump like a "jump across the river" contest using two ropes as banks of the river—gradually move the ropes further and further apart. Anyone who lands "in the water" is out.

(59) We should have an Arch in Topeka like they have in St. Louis.

(60) There has been concern expressed in the community that on exceptionally hot days the elderly persons who are without air-conditioning suffer. They could go to the bars during the hot afternoons to cool off. That is the "off season" for bars and there a lot of cool space is going to waste.

(61) When you set the school clocks forward in the spring for daylight savings time, do it at about 1 p. m. on a Monday when we want the clock to move fast, not like you have been doing it when we lose an hour's sleep.

(62) We should try to get a copy of the test that a person has to take to be a Pope. Then we could study for the test in case we ever get to take the Pope test.

The Waiver Committee—At our administrators meeting we were informed that every school in Kansas will be required to have a breakfast program unless they are granted a waiver. Our district needs to form a waiver committee to handle the situation. I thought it would be funny to suggest that bus drivers would be the most qualified to be on the waver committee because they wave at other drivers all the time. Nobody laughed.

I spent two hours stuck in my car. I couldn't get the safety belt undone so I went home and honked in the driveway, but Myra wasn't home. Then I drove to a drive-up telephone but I didn't have any change. I had no choice but to drive up to the front door of the school and honk. The students just gave me a friendly smile, waved, and went on to class. I finally caught the P.E. teacher coming in from the ball diamond, and she sent a kid out with a pair of scissors. Before cutting the belt, the kid tried the buckle and it opened right up. Enough said about that!

Chuck's Pet Cat—The elementary school had some excitement today. A part of the new and innovative science program is designed to teach children to appreciate animals. All of the classrooms have pets that the kids help care for. Last night about five pet rats escaped and spent the evening eating the wires that run to and from computers. The teachers didn't notice this until some of the kids had turned on the computers and ruined most of the programs on the hard drives. Now the staff is faced with making the decision of whether or not to set traps to catch the pet rats. The kids are siding with the rats. This whole episode reminds me of the time, years ago when I was an elementary school principal, that a kindergarten student brought a kitten to show-and-tell. After the kitten had been proudly shown, the teacher was ready to move on to another topic. She sent the student and the kitten to my office with a note asking me to telephone the student's mother and ask her to come over to the school to pick up the kitten. The mother acted quite irritated that I had called her and informed me in no uncertain terms that her family had no pet kitten and she would NOT come over to get someone else's cat. We figured out that the student had picked up the cat when he was walking to school. We fed the cat and fixed up a nice place in my office for it to rest while I walked all over the neighborhood going door to door asking if anyone had lost a cat. No one claimed the cat or wanted it. We advertised in the newspaper and worked through the PTA, but nobody knew where the cat had come from. It was clear that I now owned a cat! Thinking that animal lovers would praise me for doing so, I took it to the humane shelter. The lady who works there gave me a lecture about animal rights, said she wasn't in the business of killing cats, and only agreed to take the cat off my hands after I agreed to pay $25 to cover expenses. Our kindergarten teacher thought all of this was funny and to this day loves to tell anyone who will listen about Chuck's pet cat.

Fire Drills—The weather was great today so I decided that it would be a good time to have our monthly fire drill. I learned the hard way not to sound the alarm at the very beginning of the hour when students are dressing for physical education, or worse yet at the end of the period when they are showering. I waited until just the right moment and turned the key that starts the alarm. Everything went just as rehearsed. The students left the building quietly and even stayed in single file rows as they walked rapidly out their assigned exits. We had sounded the signal to return to class and were recording the drill on the sheet on the wall in the office when we smelled something burning. Then we saw smoke coming out of the Home Economics room door. The cooking class had a fine meal cooking when the alarm sounded and had just left it on the stove to burn. We got the smoke stopped and then I asked them why they had done "such a stupid thing." The class told me that it might seem stupid to me because I knew that the fire alarm was just a drill, but at the time it seemed like the wise thing for them to do because they thought that the school was burning down. How would it look in the paper the next day if they had lost their life to save the corned beef hash? They were right so I backed off and wished them well. Fire drills can be dangerous!

Santa Claus and Principals—I knew some people who really had the Christmas spirit, but they had a hard time communicating it. They wrote on the inside of their front windows with white paint, "MERRY XMAS." They never did discover that the message was backwards when read from the outside.

On our field trip to the Rest Home, we got mixed up and led the kids in singing "Hark the Herald Angels Sing" to the tune of "Deck the Halls."

I've played the role of Santa Claus many times and always enjoyed it. It is fun to see the happy faces of the little kids and witness close-up the excitement that they feel. I found out today that mixing the role of Santa Claus with fulfilling the function of principal of a middle school doesn't mix. I had the red suit on and was doing some robust, "Ho, Ho, Hos," when I saw one of our students hit another student and heard some loud swearing. I looked around for someone to intervene and realized that my only two options were to overlook it or get involved myself. I acted more by conditioned response than after thinking it over. I went over to where the action was taking place and before I knew it, a full fledged fight had erupted. I succeeded in breaking up the fight but my beard got torn off and the Santa suit was torn badly. I made some Un-Santa type statements and decided then and there that I would never again try to play Santa where I might need to also act as principal. When someone complains about something that I do and I tell them, "Hey, I'm not Santa Claus," I mean it in more ways than one.

Breakfast Visitor—A dad comes in to visit school every day just at free breakfast time. He always acts surprised when offered a cup of coffee and whatever the kids are eating that day, but he reluctantly accepts. His dream is to "Move way out to Wyoming and open up a combination gas station-grocery store, and live on the second floor." He doesn't want to live where there are many people because then someone would always be bothering him. Some far off place would be fine. He figures that he would have free gas and free food and a place to live for nothing; what more could a person want.

He called me at home to tell me that he was going to check his son out of school the next day because he had "Inherited a fortune—$562." He had bought a car and was going to take the trip that he had wanted to take all of his life. The car was "in great shape, the only thing it doesn't have is a gas tank and I'm going to weld one on tonight, and we'll leave in the morning." He hadn't decided whether he and his family would go to Arkansas or Wyoming. "We'll just get on the road and decide after we've been going a few days," he said.

Stuck In The Elevator—I am a member of our district health committee. We met last night. The meeting was on the third floor of the Central Office building. It is understood that those of us on that committee should promote exercise so I usually walk up the stairs when I am heading to a health committee meeting. Last night no one was around, and I was feeling lazy so I got on the elevator. I was thinking how smart I was to use technology and how dumb others were to walk up the steps. Then I thought that maybe there are some times that it isn't best to use technology even though it is available. Maybe the mind and body both need exercise, and sometimes it would be best to exercise them instead of using technology. Our math department might want to take another look at how often kids use calculators. Then, when the elevator was between floors, the power went off! It was pitch black and completely silent for what seemed like an eternity. It wasn't my physical safety that concerned me at all. I was worried about how I would explain to the public why I was on the elevator in the first place. Fortunately, I got out without anyone even knowing about it. I was telling Ole about it today. He consoled me by saying that something like that wouldn't hurt my public image because people have come to expect that type of thing from me. I don't know how he could think something like that about me.

The most radical thing that I have done in months is to occasionally throw caution to the wind and order the hash browns, eggs, and bacon special for breakfast instead of my usual conservative oatmeal and toast. Anyway, Ole has been known to make a mistake once in a while himself, like the time he replaced the screw that holds on the sun visor support in his car with a larger screw and it went right through the car roof and outside. It looked like a unicorn. I suggested that he might want to fill the resulting hole by pounding a golf tee into it.

Some Things Are Worth Standing Up For—Ole and I were discussing the fact that there are some things in life that are important enough that a guy has to take a stand for or against them. Ole said that he was not proud to report that he had recently given in on two of the three things that he had always put in that category. He reluctantly admitted that yesterday he drank a diet soft drink. He had been tricked into it! He pulled it up out of the ice in the cooler and never read the label. He said that he had always felt that it was just wrong to pay to drink something that has as its main claim that it has no calories and no caffeine. That is too negative a way to live. A few weeks ago he had unknowingly listened to FM radio. He had always thought that FM radio was Communist inspired, un-American, and would never stand the test of time. He was proud to be able to say that he had not fallen on the third thing that he has taken a stand against, corn dogs. He went on to tell how real Americans eat hot dogs in a bun at ball games and asked if God didn't want a wiener to be in a bun, why he had created the hot dog bun? Now it is the goal of all of us on the staff to figure out a way that we can trick Ole into eating a corn dog. Ole said that the first time he saw Dolly Parton on TV, he got up and adjusted his rabbit ears antenna because he couldn't believe his eyes. He still has some serious doubts about whether there is really a Dolly Parton. He thinks the whole image could be a hoax, like an adult Santa Claus myth. After all nobody he knows personally has ever seen her in person. He also devoted about half an hour to complaining about how negative his priest is. "All he ever talks about is sin. A person can be perfectly happy when he goes into church, and when he comes out he is bound to feel like a terrible sinner." It is a strange coincidence that, on the same day, Mike had been complaining that his priest was too positive and Pollyanna type and that reminded him of school where we constantly preach about "improving the self-concept and everyone can learn." He said he hears that stuff all week in school and wants to get away from it on Sundays.

Snakes—One of the worst things that can happen to a Swede happened to Ole last night. His wife was dusting the inside of the piano and found a six foot long snake skin on top of the wooden hammers. They have no idea how long it has been there or where the snake is now. To put it mildly, his whole family is up-tight about the situation.

A few summers ago my son Steve picked up what he thought was a garden hose to get a drink, and it wasn't a hose at all. It was a big black snake. He dropped it right away, and we started yelling for Myra (just a habit I guess because she is just as afraid of snakes as we are). The snake slithered over and started going around and around my Aunt Esther's legs. Esther, my favorite aunt, was recuperating from cateract surgery on her eyes and was sitting in a lawn chair on the porch. She couldn't look down so she just got up calmly and walked into the house, the snake curled around her legs. After we got it off Aunt Esther, a neighbor boy killed the snake with an axe and we saved it for a few days to show anyone who would look at it. All of this didn't phase Aunt Esther.

Our science teacher loves snakes and keeps lots of them in his classroom. I am always careful of what I lean on when I go into his classroom to visit. The snakes get out of their cages once in a while and we get a kid or the science teacher to retrieve them. It is terrible to go down a dark hallway on a weekend and not know for sure if I will step on a snake. That has happened several times. I guess it goes with the job, but no one told me that when I was in graduate school.

The grandkids had lots of fun last weekend playing out in the driveway. They didn't understand what they were doing so I just gritted my teeth and laughed it off. Some large cracks had developed in the asphalt so I had filled them with a clear caulking. The kids pealed the caulking out and left it lying there in the driveway. At first glance it looked like a snake skin. I told them to watch out for snakes and showed them the "snake skins" that I had found. They asked me why snake skins would have been in the cracks where they had found it. Another learning experience.

Career Night—We held our annual career night last night. We had over 50 different careers represented. The doctor got a little bent out of shape when I asked him if he would mind taking a look at a mole on my hip. One of the teachers told me that it could be a "melanoma." Ole said that he thought he went to grade school with a girl by that name. The doctor tried to be nice but he refused by saying that I should make an appointment to come to his office. What would happen if I said that to a parent the next time one of them stops me at the grocery store and asks me about school? Lots of kids interviewed the mortician and asked, "Do employees get a discount?" At least they will do me less harm if they end up working in that profession in the future than if they work as doctors or lawyers and then cause me to need a mortician.

Ole Feeds The Wildlife—Ole told me that for the past month he has been pouring the garbage outside in his backyard to draw wildlife. He reasoned that it is silly to waste something that some hungry creature could eat. Yesterday his wife put an end to the practice when she looked out in the backyard and saw a whole family of skunks eating the popcorn that Ole had put out there. She yelled at Ole. Ole went outside and confronted the skunks, they confronted Ole, and Ole did something he rarely does. He has changed his philosophy.

Plumbers—Plumbers charge so much that I always at least try to fix things myself when I have a plumbing problem (not me personally that is, but in my house). I have never gotten by with only one trip to the hardware store. No matter how careful I am, I always either get the wrong size or forget to get something vital. When I find that I can't fix something, or after I have made matters worse, I give up and reluctantly call in an expert.

My daughter and son-in-law had a plumbing problem. Two toilets wouldn't drain. I told them I would "take a look at them." I ran a 25 foot long "plumber's snake" up through one of them. How was I to know that (1) the "snake" would not go down the drain pipe but instead would go up and out of the toilet in the bathroom on the other side of the wall and (2) that my daughter would be sitting on that toilet and get stuck by the twisting "snake" as it came up out of that toilet? Next time I'll let them pay for a plumber. I guess plumbers charge less than doctors.

Attendance Problems—A student called the school at 8 a.m. yesterday and told the secretary, "Billy Wilson is sick today and won't be at school." The secretary recognized the voice to be Billy Wilson himself. She said, "Billy, let me talk to your mom." Billy replied, "This IS my mom and she ain't here, but my fever just busted so I'll probably be able to come to school tomorrow."

Two Hours In A Cottonwood Tree—One of the objectives of Outdoor Education is to provide the opportunity for kids to experience first hand the beauty and marvel of nature. Unfortunately, when several hundred city kids are transported to the outdoors by a dozen big yellow school buses, all most of them experience is each other. Instead of eating lunch alone in a meadow under a tree and observing wildlife, they sit in the shade of a school bus and talk to each other. With tongue in cheek, the staff demonstrates how the native Americans opened their plastic potato chip bags before they were influenced by the white man. They also lead the group in chanting "an old Indian religious ritual," "stay low, go slow" as they climb up and down hills. Formal instruction is interrupted on occasion to look for some poor soul's glasses when they fall into the creek. Ole found his a year later and down stream about a mile.

Most people would agree that the most enjoyable time experienced during an Outdoor Education overnight camping trip is in the late evening when the entire group gathers around the campfire and sings songs and tells stories. Our desired outcomes in those situations stem from the content areas of language arts and music. We would never admit that we are just having a great time. Much of the learning that we remember the longest takes place when we have fun. Although we should know better, we eventually get around to telling ghost stories. The kids never tire of hearing stories about the "Albino Lady of Rochester Cemetery," "Harry Hand," and "The Old Man." We get the kids scared and that, along with being away from home and sleeping on the hard ground, causes them to have difficulty sleeping. Scaring kids does not match up with sound educational practice and philosophy, but then some of the most fun things that we do don't. So we do it anyway.

On this particular night we planned to perpetuate the "Cottonwood Tree Monster" hoax. My fellow teacher told me to climb up high in a huge cottonwood tree. After a while he would tell the story and lead the group under the tree and I would scare them by letting out loud noises. I climbed high up into the tree and got comfortable on a large limb. At first I enjoyed the peace and quiet and listening to the music that resulted when the wind hit the cottonwood leaves. Looking at the full moon and a sky full of glittering stars made the experience even more pleasant. After about a half hour I started to wish the group would show up as I was getting a little tired of sitting there on the branch. An hour passed and then two hours. I finally decided that some kind of emergency must have come up and that I better go check the situation out. As I walked into the light of the camp fire the kids saw me and they yelled out in unison, "Did you have a good time sitting in the tree, Mr. Sodergren?" Then it hit me! The trick had been on me, and I had fallen for it hook, line and sinker. I had to admit it was funny and since that time, I have returned the favor by arranging for over a dozen of my co-workers to experience sitting in a tree. The only difference was that none of them took two hours to figure out something was wrong. Persistence and patience are virtues that in this case didn't pay off.

Casting Demonstration—Once on a weekend outing, I was demonstrating to my own kids how to cast a fishing line. I baited the hook with a huge grasshopper, pulled the fishing pole back, and cast with all of my might. The fish hook came forward and stuck in my ear. At the same time the bobber hit me on the back of my head and nearly knocked me out. The kids thought all of this was hilarious. Looking back on it now I know that the smart thing to do would have been to immediately remove the grasshopper from the hook but I wasn't thinking clearly and drove all the way home with the "grasshopper earring." The kids laughed every time they looked at me–which was most of the time. When we got home I had Myra remove the grasshopper, push the hook on through my ear lobe, and cut the hook with a wire cutter. We then went to the hospital to get a tetanus shot. The nurse asked me to give the details about what happened. That was embarrassing!

Gambling—Once our family was traveling through Nevada. I wanted to teach the kids the evils of gambling. I told them to watch while I put a nickel into a slot machine and see how stupid it was to waste your money doing such a dumb thing. I hit the jackpot! Some lessons don't work.

New Telephone Number—A student came to the office window yesterday and told the secretary that her parents had a new telephone number. The secretary was busy and so she gave the student a piece of paper and a pencil and said, "Write that down." The student wrote on the paper, "My parents have a new telephone number," and walked down the hall to class. The secretary has no idea who the kid was.

Basketball Tryouts—Last week our basketball coach put up a sign about tryouts. I accused him of purposely putting the sign up on the wall so high that only tall kids could read it so he might be able to avoid cutting so many kids because only the tall ones would come out. It all backfired on him when he made the mistake of saying in the announcements that he was having a "short boys basketball meeting" because only short kids attended.

Confidentiality—We received a notice that a seminar was going to be held about confidentiality. I figured that we should practice what we preach and kept the notice confidential. No one attended the meeting. We joked that we should keep student records in the counselor's office confidential by putting them in camouflage colored folders so no one will see them. It is interesting that the Army changed the look of camouflage from the "jungle" to "desert" during the Desert Storm war. If they are going to drive trucks down a highway, maybe camouflage should be highway color.

Dog Bites Billy—The family of one of our students had a dog for over 12 years. It had become a much loved member of the family. The dad came home from work one evening and read a note that said, "Dog bit Billy. Had to get rid of him." The dad said that at first he didn't know whether they got rid of the dog or Billy. Earlier in the year Billy told me, "My dog had four puppies, we would have had five but two died." The mom had told us, "We give Billy responsibilities at home, like we told him 'It's your responsibility to feed the dog and if you don't do it, he'll just die and that's YOUR problem'." We told them that it might be the dog's problem also. They told me that they bought a toy saxophone at the toy store that plays "real music." I don't know what other kind of music there is. We told them we want to teach Billy "higher level thinking." They said that they didn't think he could do that because he wasn't tall enough.

Roller Skating—A lady with no income whose kid is on free lunch came to our school roller skating party last night and rented skates for a baby that can't even walk. We had met with her earlier in the week to set up an Individual Educational Plan for her middle school aged daughter. The girl's career goal a year ago was to be a roller skating waitress, but now she wants to be a doctor.

Modern Version of the Boy's Town Motto—I chastised a kid today for hitting another kid. He replied, "It's okay, Mr. Sodergren, he's my brother." I guess that must be the modern version of the old Boy's Town motto, "He ain't heavy, Father, he's my brother." With that attitude it is no wonder we have so much family violence and spousal abuse in the community.

Tumbleweeds—Myra and I noticed some tumbleweeds blowing north one day, and then a few days later we saw some blowing across the road from north to south. We discussed the possibility that these could be the same tumbleweeds. I know that those people who study the migratory habits of birds use a practice called banding to identify birds. I suggested that we could try banding tumbleweeds so we could know for sure if we see the same one twice. We might even write up our findings in a scholarly article and get it published. Myra told me that if I did that she would disown me. Her relatives in California have always wondered why she would leave sunny California to live in what they perceived as a lonesome, barren, prairie called Kansas. Their idea of Kansas was what they got from watching "Gunsmoke" on television and they always felt pity for Myra having to live in a place like that. Any connection of me with tumbleweeds would only strengthen that view. We decided to forget all about the topic. I suggested maybe we could study grasshoppers. That idea didn't go over too well either.

I Can Put Them To Sleep—Sometimes parents have a difficult time convincing their kids that it is in their best interest to go to sleep. We have all witnessed crying infants that need to sleep but fight it to the end. It is at times like this that I take over. When I start talking, kids have a tendency to doze off. All I have to do is start telling about how hot it was during the first summer of my life, the summer of '34, and how we adjusted to it and what I did in the Navy, and everyone present falls asleep. Over the years I have developed a soothing and calming tone of voice. I guess it is a result of all of the lectures I have made in my office on changing behavior and as an American History teacher before I became an administrator. I told Ole about this and suggested that perhaps I should become a radio or TV newsman. He said that they wouldn't hire a guy that is so dull and boring that he puts people to sleep when he talks. They want people to stay awake until the news is over. He's probably just jealous. I think I'm a pretty exciting and dynamic guy myself. Like the narrator of nature films we all remember.

Only Do Math In School—Myra went into the grocery store to buy only one item so I stayed in the car with the grandkids. I pointed out a sign that said, "Open 6:00 a.m.-12:00 p.m." and asked them to figure out how long the store is open each day. They said, "Stop it, Grandpa. We aren't in school now. That's the only place we do math."

Fishing and Watermelons—Last summer we took our youngest granddaughter, Audrey, fishing. While she wasn't looking, I put a fish that I had caught on her hook and told her to pull it in. She got all excited and we took a great picture of the experience. It reminded us of the time years ago when we bought a watermelon at the store and placed it on top of the watermelon vine in our garden where none had been the previous day. Our kids got excited and couldn't understand how such a grand melon could grow overnight. The trick backfired when they expected more of the same.

Enjoying the Summertime—It's hard to remember to switch from summer language to school year language each year when school starts. Now and then an "ain't" will slip out, but gradually the adjustment always occurs. I quit smoking my pipe on June 1st. Then instead of smoking, I ate anything in sight. This caused me to add about 30 pounds of fat around my mid-section. I experienced the shock of my life when we looked at the video tape of our vacation in Minnesota. There it was for everyone to see. I looked for the world like a big white whale emerging from the water. I knew that I had put on a few pounds but I never dreamed that I looked like that! I had to do something about this. I did two things; first, I went on a strict diet, and second, I've stayed away from video tape cameras and mirrors from that day on. During the summer I broke six lawn chairs. That is a new record. The entire family kept track and each event was duly noted and celebrated. I looked for an 800 number on the chairs so I could call in and complain, but it's probably best that I couldn't find it and make a fool out of myself.

Oral Reading—Myra doesn't get too mad when I practice my oral reading by reading the high school football scores and write-ups out of the newspaper. But when I read the obituaries out loud, and get louder and louder, word for word—with emphasis, and make comments about nicknames and ages, it gets to the point that she lets me know of her irritation. I go on to read the letters to the editor, the way they are meant to be read, out loud and mad, but I do it in the bathroom by myself.

A Slot Type Guy In A Phillips Type of World—Modern gadgets always give me fits. When it comes to screwdrivers and other tools, I'm kind of a slot type of guy in a Phillips type of world. I took the grandkids out to the golf driving range today and put the required amount of money in the golf ball dispenser machine so they could hit a few balls. We had a terrible mess because we didn't know that we had to put a basket under where the golf balls come out of the machine. Balls rolled all over the place.

Once I broke a self service soft drink dispenser machine at the fast food section of the mall when I hit it too hard on the wrong spot. If I had been shorter maybe I would have noticed the little lever underneath the plastic sign.

I think someone stays up nights dreaming up new and creative places to put flush valves on urinals and drinking fountains. Last week I pushed every spot on a urinal after using it only to discover, as I walked away from it, that it flushed automatically. It scared the daylights out of me! Ole and I never did figure out what triggers it. We spit into it, poured water into it, and even ran our hands down near the water, but nothing happened. And then as we gave up and walked away, it flushed again. It almost makes a person believe that someone has been hired to watch through a hole in the wall and scare us poor mortals.

Farmer Wanabees—Many of our school patrons are "farmer wanabees." They live and work in town, but they drive pickup trucks and wear ball caps with seed company ads on them.

Measles—Yesterday didn't start out very well. A kid was diagnosed as having measles. He told the school nurse that he had gone out and got the measles on purpose so he could come to school and give them to me. He was upset when I told him that I had had the measles when I was a child and was now immune.

Ivy—I suggested to the staff that we could plant ivy all around the school building to make it a place where high level thinking takes place. This worked for Harvard and Yale and the other schools in the Ivy league so we should give it a try. Ole said that he had heard that a school in western Kansas had ivy growing all over it but had to cut it down. It turns out it was poison ivy. We decided at our staff meeting to take "before" and "after" pictures of teachers. We thought that these pictures would prove the stress we are under and convince the public that we deserve a raise in pay.

After school I took the grandkids to the zoo. We all went into the rain forest building. The animals are all loose in there. I was looking up at the birds when I stepped on a very large lizard. This startled me so much that I sprained my ankle. Then, to make matters worse, when I was bent over lifting two of the smaller kids up to see the alligators, my glasses slid off my nose and fell into the water. The alligators just sat there motionless looking like they would love to see me try to retrieve the glasses—sort of a "go ahead make my day" stare. We had to find a zoo worker to get my glasses.

My son, Steve, gave us a new telephone answering machine for Christmas. I really made a fool out of myself when I tried to use it without reading the directions closely enough. Myra had recorded a real cute statement for people to hear when they called us and we weren't home. She also figured out a way to leave a message for me when I come home and she has gone somewhere. When I came home and the "message" light was blinking, I pushed the button and heard her message telling me where she went and when she would be home. It was so neat that I thought I would be cute and leave a message for her. I recorded a message something like this: "Hi, this is your sweet little lover boy Chucky. I'm not home now, but if you are a nice little girl, I'll give you a big kiss when I see you. Over and out and I can't wait to give you a big hug." I didn't know that I had hit the wrong button and that my smart aleck message had replaced the message that everyone who called our house heard. This went on for several days. I noticed that I was getting a few little smiles from people who don't normally smile much at me, but I had no idea why until I called home myself. I about died when I heard my own voice. The message sounded real stupid, not at all cute like I thought it would to Myra. I made up some excuse to go home immediately to erase the evidence before anyone else could hear it. I wondered how many parents had called. How embarrassing!

I thought I would do something nice for my secretary on "Secretaries Day" so I wrote a long letter to her telling her how great she is. She appreciated the content of the letter but it sort of ruined the day when I asked her to type it for me. Yesterday was such a stressful day that she said that she was looking forward to her dental appointment after school.

Visiting the Spanish Class—I went down to visit the Spanish class today. The teacher said that the kids had really gotten into hitting the pinata since they made one that was a likeness of my head. I'm sure that he was just joking, at least I hope so.

Outdoor Education— The "Tractor in the Lake Lesson"—Most of "Seaman Acres," our outdoor education lab, is maintained in its natural condition. We mow some small areas so staff and students can move around a little easier. I had almost completed mowing for the day but I wanted to make one last loop down next to the lake to cut out several tall weeds that had grown up on the water's edge. I drove the tractor toward the lake and then turned the steering wheel to drive horizontally next to the lake. The front wheels slid in the mud and the tractor continued chugging toward the lake. It is easy, in hindsight, to second guess my reactions and recite several possible alternative actions that I should have taken, but at the time I just froze and drove the tractor straight into the lake. I jumped off as we hit the water and climbed back onto the shore. I stood there watching the oil rise to the water's surface. About a foot of the exhaust pipe stuck out of the water. The water kind of sizzled on the exhaust pipe and then all was quiet. It had been a close call and I should have been thankful for my own safety but being thankful was the last thing on my mind. I thought about Ted Kennedy and how he had recently driven off a bridge and a young lady had died. I thought about the possibility of taking off to Mexico or some other far-off land and being in exile the rest of my life. Maybe I could deny that I knew anything about how the tractor got into the lake. Then I looked up and saw Ole walking along the path that I had just completed mowing. He was leading about twenty kids and they were all happily whistling the theme to "Bridge Over the River Kwai" and "Hi Ho, Hi Ho, it's Off to Work We Go." They had been watching me mow and were now coming to check on my safety. They thought my performance was hilarious. Ole and I went up to the camp headquarters and drove a bus down to the accident scene. We tied a rope from the back of the bus to the tractor and pulled it out of the water. The tractor looked like a wet dog that had just emerged from the water and was about to start shaking. The only thing left to do now was to call the superintendent and tell him what I had done. I dreaded calling him but thought I had better get it over with. He said, "You what?" and I repeated the story with my voice quaking. After he asked me if I was okay, there was a long silence on the phone, and he said, "We'll contact the transportation department and have them drain the oil and take care of it." I said, "I'm sorry, and I'll pay for any damage." He replied, "There is no need to do that. You were doing what you were supposed to do. If the tractor had been damaged because you were doing something that you shouldn't have been doing, it would be a different story. I'm only glad you're okay." I learned much from the incident and have related the story many times to staff who are concerned about whether I will back them when the going gets tough.

The Ill Fated Canoe Trip—One of my friends was the director of recreational programs at a penal institution for young men. We discussed the merits of taking about a dozen of these young criminals on a ten-mile canoe trip down one of the beautiful small rivers that meander across the plains of Kansas. On only rare occasions had many of them been out of the hostile urban environment, where they had been born and gotten into trouble. We thought that an encounter with nature might help them to change their very negative attitudes.

The school district supplied six canoes that were used in the Outdoor Education program and the penal institution agreed to supply staff to supervise the activity and prevent the young men from escaping. We transported the group to the site on the river where the trip would begin. I gave them exactly the same lecture on "merging your soul and silently soaking up the wonders of nature" that I had given to begin many other trips by students of our school. After some very fundamental instruction and a demonstration on canoeing technique and safety, we were ready to begin our great experiment.

Much to our surprise, the young men reacted just as they had been conditioned to act in the urban ghetto. They knocked canoes over, hit each other with paddles, yelled and swore loudly, and splashed water on each other during the entire ten-mile trip down the river. Many of the aluminum canoes were dented, literally all of the paddles broken, and it took the staff at the institution over a week to sort out all of the assaults and who caused what damage to the property of farmers along the way. Sometimes theory and reality don't completely match up.

Our Family Trip in the Great Outdoors—All winter long I looked at a pretty picture on the wall of my classroom showing a warm summer day in the woods with a nice quiet stream flowing. It seemed like a perfect setting to enjoy nature and I dreamed of taking a month long trip the next summer to do just that with my wife and four kids. We started packing the Rambler station wagon a week before we were to leave and had a well planned place for every item. We studied a map of Kansas to pick out a place to spend our first night on our dream trip. We decided on a spot in western Kansas where a tree symbol on the map indicated there was a small county state lake. The trip to the camping spot went fine, and we enjoyed singing songs and playing travel type games that we had read about. We arrived at the site, which was about ten miles off of the paved roads, and noticed that nobody else was camping there. The "lake" was not much more than a pond according to eastern Kansas standards. We set up the tent, ate our first meal in the great outdoors, and went for a short walk. We noticed some dark clouds on the western horizon but didn't think much about them. When we got back to the tent it started to rain. Then the wind started to blow. The rain got heavier and the wind velocity increased so we thought we better get everything inside the tent. We soon decided we better listen to the radio to see if we could learn anything about the weather. We went across the entire AM and FM dial on our radio and found only one station. That station reported that there was "grapefruit sized hail" falling at a location just to our west and then signed off the air because it only operated during the daylight hours. We got the kids into the car and threw all of our camping gear (now very wet and muddy) into the back of the station wagon. Myra drove because I had to hang on the back of the car and push the car much of the time to keep it going in the mud and to keep it from sliding off the road. The rain came down so hard that Myra could hardly see. She was so nervous that her foot shook on the gas pedal which made the car go in spurts. I was covered with mud from head to foot. We finally got to a hard surfaced road and the rain let up some. We pulled into a motel after midnight and I'm sure the manager would have never rented us a room if he had seen me.

The rest of the trip we either stayed in established campgrounds with lots of other people, with relatives, or in motels. We all suffered severe sunburn from staying on the beach too long in southern California and had a scare when we got separated on the cable cars in San Francisco. Luckily we were reunited on fisherman's wharf. I learned the hard way that a 25 cent investment to wash off the salt water after swimming in the Great Salt Lake is money well spent. By the time we were about a hundred miles down the road, salt seemed to find every sore on my body, especially on the area I sit on, and made life quite miserable. After losing a wheel bearing in Arizona, picking ticks off our bodies, worrying about the little kids falling in a rushing mountain stream in Colorado where we camped down wind from a massive cattle feed lot, and buying a tire on an Indian reservation in New Mexico to replace the one that blew out, we finally got back home. The nature picture on the wall in my classroom didn't show any odor, mud, mosquitoes, or ticks and there was no hint that the temperature might not always be comfortable. We had gained a new appreciation for indoor living in Topeka, Kansas. Sometimes theory and reality don't completely match up.

The Smoky River Festival—Every year Myra and I spend the second weekend of June at the Smoky Valley River Festival in Salina. That is my idea of a perfect vacation. The park is filled with great art, music, and common Kansas folks having a wonderful time. We can leave our lawn chairs and other possessions to walk around and look at the craft booths and be confident that everything will still be there when we return. Once in a while we need to move the lawn chairs because the sun has shifted and we want to be in the shade or because we want to move to a different stage but that is about the extent of the stress felt. I noticed that "caning" was listed on the festival program this year and looked forward to seeing some poor soul get punished by being beat by canes like they do in Singapore. Much to my surprise that program dealt with refurbishing old chairs.

Of course it is easier to talk about not allowing kids to get to you than it is to practice it. I am reminded of an incident that happened years ago when I was working in the district Outdoor Education program. Ole, George, and I had a practice of stopping at a restaurant after work for a cup of coffee and to talk about the day's activities. They told me about a kid that had irritated them so much that day that Ole turned around on the school bus and stuck a stocking in the kid's mouth. I told them that they needed to be constantly in control of what they do and that they shouldn't act in such an immature manner. The next day I asked the same kid to help me unload a canoe. He told me, "Unload it yourself, mister, I'm not your slave." Before I knew it I had the kid by his shirt and had started to unload on him. Then I looked up and saw Ole and George watching and laughing their heads off. They really enjoyed themselves over coffee.

No Free Lunch—Yesterday our elementary principal held a staff meeting to address the problem of teachers not paying for their lunches as promptly as he thought they should. They always paid, but sometimes they forgot their money and paid the next day. He said there could be no excuse for that to happen and went on to point out that they could not expect to eat anywhere else in North Topeka without paying on the spot. Why should it be any different at the school? This morning he ate breakfast at the cafe and when he went to pay the bill, he realized that he had forgotten his billfold and didn't have any money. Of course they know him there and were happy to let him pay later but not without some ridicule. It seems that some of his teachers had told them of his "No Money, No Eat" message of the day before.

Ole's Name Change—Ole told me that when his ancestors were coming over to America from Sweden back in the 1880s they changed their last name from Anderson to Johnson because there were so many Andersons. That doesn't make sense to me because it seems to me that there are more Johnsons than Andersons. My ancestors were named Anderson and were smart enough to change their name to Sodergren on the ship coming over from Sweden. Maybe Ole and I are related. I better remember to ask him what ship his ancestors came over on.

Right Lane Driving—Back in the 1960s my mom and dad took an automobile trip to the eastern part of the United States to see the big cities that they had only read about. We could hardly wait to hear their impressions of New York City and Chicago. When they got back home, they reported that they had by-passed all of the big cities because the traffic went faster on the by-pass routes. That tactic would have been great if their objective had been to get someplace fast, but it kind of defeated the purpose if they wanted to really see big cities. We did the opposite thing last year when we were returning home from Minnesota. We took the three lane business route through Des Moines, Iowa, so we could see the downtown and capitol building. I decided to play it safe and drive in the middle lane. I always try to stay in either the right or center lane when I am driving a car, taking a stand on social and financial issues, or using the urinal. Before I realized what was happening, the fast lane to my left ended and I had a terrible time getting over in the right lane. For a short time I was in the far left or fast lane. That same thing happens to me on occasion on social and financial issues. I take a position that I think is clearly a middle-of-the-road or conservative position and it turns out to cost tax money or promote social concerns that are usually identified with left wing politics. Common sense creates strange bedfellows.

Size 42 Days—I'm afraid that I have been gaining weight. A few years ago I was very comfortable wearing size 42 undershorts. We bought lots of them when they were on sale. I have unfortunately increased my belly size so when I buy undershorts now, I buy size 44. Being the cheapskate that I am, I don't want to throw away my perfectly good sized 42 undershorts so I continue to wear them on some days. I overheard some of the staff say that they could tell when it was a "44 day" because I was much easier to get along with than on "42 days." Maybe we can find someone who has grown from a size 40 to size 42 and would be interested in purchasing some used underwear. I wonder what the sales clerk will think when I buy about 18 pair of new size 44 undershorts. I will tell her that they are a birthday present for a friend.

Dreams—Ole, told me that he has been teaching Reading so long that he now dreams in chapters. Tomorrow night's dream will start on page 29. Sometimes he can hardly wait to go to sleep to see what is going to happen next. Other times, when he woke up just in time to keep alive the night before, he is worried about going to sleep.

The kids in the commons at noon and I agreed that if you are falling in a dream and land, you are dead. The rumor had gotten around that it is against the law to go out Halloweening any time except within a week of Halloween. Someone else had heard that it is against the law to open an umbrella in the house. We discussed these issues for a while and then a seventh grade boy said that his grandpa told him that if you burp, hick-up, and relieve yourself of gas at the same time, you will die. Another kid said that the three things were sneeze, hick-up, and burp. They started arguing and almost came to blows. I told them they should look it up in the encyclopedia or ask the doctor the next time they saw him. I wasn't convinced that either version was true but decided to do neither if I could help it. At least when the kids are discussing higher level concepts like these, they are not doing what comes natural for them—tapping each other on the shoulder and then looking the other way, pushing the guy on the end of the bench off, and chasing each other.

Parent Complaint—A mom called to complain that the Physical Education teacher made her son work so hard that "his fat was tired and ached." She said we should take care of this now and "nip it in the butt."

No "Boys" Restrooms? A parent of a new seventh grade student called me at home to complain that we didn't have any boys restrooms. Her son came home and reported that he had seen lots of men's restrooms, the same number of women's restrooms, and in between all of these, restrooms for custodians, but none for boys. We changed the signs. The mother claimed to be an expert on middle schools because she had spent five years in one. Don't want to overlook advice from someone that knowledgeable.

Learning To Write A Letter Of Application—We are fortunate to have a very competent and creative seventh grade English teacher. In yesterday's class her objective was to have the students write a letter of application for a job. She cut out the "help wanted" section of the want ads from the daily paper and made an overhead transparency to use in her class to motivate the students. It wasn't until late in the class period that she discovered what some of the kids had been giggling about. The column next to the "help wanted" was the Personals which included such statements as "If you want fantastic girls call...." She had been projecting that in her lesson right next to the Help Wanted. I thought it was funny and nobody complained, but she was embarrassed anyway.

Conditioning and Association—Over the past few years we have had so many complaints about the smell in our school restrooms that we decided to try to do something about the smell. My response to these complaints in the past had been to make some comment like, "Considering what people do in there, it would be a miracle if it didn't smell bad in there." We decided to purchase the services of an air freshener expert. He put in an air freshening system that allowed us to pick the smell we wanted each time he came to change the canister. We have enjoyed the smell of lots of different kinds of flowers and exotic places. For a while I really liked these smells but recently I have come to associate these smells with restrooms. We had some flowers in the house that Myra thought smelled great but they smelled like school restrooms to me.

I did some serious thinking today about the possibility that smells are not good or bad in and of themselves, but instead are good or bad because of what we associate with them. I have heard that cancer patients get nauseated when they just smell the chemicals that are used in chemotherapy after they have experienced them once. On the other hand, I know that skunk smell is bad regardless of who smells it. So much for philosophy.

First Football Practice—Today was the first day of football practice for seventh grade boys. Yesterday the coach told the boys that if they are out for football they must go to bed at 10 p.m. This morning I received a telephone call from a parent who said that her boy found it difficult to stay up that late and wondered if he could have permission to go to bed earlier. These boys have never had a football uniform on, let alone played the game. The coaches noticed one boy out in the middle of the practice field lying on his back and grimacing in agonizing pain. At first they couldn't figure out what was wrong with him. After a short conversation with him and inspecting his uniform, it was determined that his thigh pads were far too big and every time he took a step they functioned like a pair of scissors on his crotch area. He was issued a smaller pair of thigh pads and his football career took a sudden turn to the bright side.

Our Natural Competitive Spirit—Most of us have a natural competitive spirit that drives us to try to be one up on each other. Today in the teachers lounge we started talking about and showing the scars that we had accumulated on our bodies over the years. Each scar had a story behind it and its owner told about it with passion. I told about the scar on my middle finger that I got in 1956 when my mother-in-law slammed the car door on it. Ole then showed us the scar on his leg that resulted from his knee operation. He even invited us over to his house to watch the operation on video-tape. Bob showed us the stump of his finger and told in detail how the rest of it got cut off. Mike told us how he got the large scar on his rear end and promised to show it to us if we would walk down the hall to the restroom. I was about to counter with my appendectomy and hernia scar when Don put me in my place by pulling up his shirt to reveal a massive scar that resulted from his open-heart surgery. Wow! We were all so jealous that at that moment any one of us would have agreed to suffer terrible pain if only we could have a scar that would beat Don's and win the biggest scar contest. We had to concede defeat.

Tomorrow our topic will be bruises. The problem with discussing bruises is that they disappear and you have no proof that you even had them let alone how big they were. I would like to enter the bruise that my wife got by bumping into a rear view mirror in the parking lot last weekend, but I know that she wouldn't let me take a picture of it. I have lots of bruises on my own body but I can't remember how or where I got them.

Understanding how the natural competitive spirit drives us to do some pretty ridiculous things may help us to understand how to help kids when we observe them practicing "one-upsmanship" with each other.

Post Mother's Day Diarrhea—Every Sunday all of our kids and grandkids come over to our house after church to eat lunch together. Myra plans these meals all week and puts on a real spread! The only Sunday that we don't eat Grandma's cooking is on Mother's Day. Then we all go to some fancy local Chinese restaurant to eat.

Every Monday after Mother's Day Sunday I experience what I have come to call "post Mother's Day diarrhea." Harry Truman once said that it is a recession when your neighbor does not have a job but it is a depression when you don't have a job yourself. The same concept differentiates what should be considered "serious" diarrhea. My son joked later that he hoped that "it doesn't 'run' in the family." I told him that it definitely was in the genes (jeans). I was fortunate that I didn't have to miss any work.

I bought some flowers last Friday and gave them to Myra and wrote the following on the card that came with them, "Happy Mother's Day, from your loving husband, Chuck." She thanked me and said that it was a good thing that I put on the card which loving husband it was from. I think she was joking.

Recently when we play BINGO, I notice that Myra watches my card as well as her own. I could get upset that she has doubts about my ability to handle my card, but I have to admit that hardly a game goes by that she doesn't help me out at least once. Can't pass up help like that.

Motels—My good friend Charlie Hogan is a great country singer but he hasn't gotten far from home. He was invited out to western Kansas to sing at a small town's centennial celebration. He was excited when he told me about it later and said, "Gosh, Chuck, they put us up in the fanciest motel you can imagine. Why there was a bathroom in every room!" Charlie judges how smart a person is not by IQ but by how they do in the TV games "Jeopardy" and "Wheel of Fortune." He claims his wife is the smartest woman alive.

I guess some people who travel a great deal get tired of staying in motels, but I still get as excited as a kid at a carnival when we stay at a motel. There is an old axiom in sports that says you should go for the win on the road and for a tie at home. I have my own axiom when it comes to staying in motels: take a bath at home and a shower on the road. This is because at home I always like to lie in hot water with everything but my belly button covered and my legs up high on the bathroom wall so the big veins in my legs and feet will drain. Last summer I was ready to step into the motel shower and was thinking that I needed to put some shampoo on my head but I needed to wet my head first. I remembered that Ole and I were just talking the week before about how stupid it was to put on shampoo labels, "wet your hair before applying." Nobody is so stupid that they would need to read the label to know how to use shampoo! I wet my hair and rubbed in the whole plastic bottle full of the complimentary shampoo that Myra handed me. For some reason it didn't lather up. Maybe I needed to rub it in more. Lo and behold, it was hand lotion not shampoo. Maybe reading labels isn't so dumb after all. At least my whole body was now soft and shouldn't itch all day.

Then I went to put some deodorant under my arms. We had forgotten to pack my regular macho man's wide stick so I had to use Myra's. It said on the label it will make "a lady smell beautiful all day." It might have been my imagination, but it seemed to me that tough looking guys looked at me in a funny way all day. Of course it could have been my slicked down hair that drew their attention too. I wonder if guys who wear wigs have a messed up one so they will look natural when the wind blows and when they first get up in the morning. I was kind of glad to check out of the motel because it seemed like everywhere I looked there was a big mirror and some ugly old guy looking back at me. Once I bumped into him and said, "Excuse me," but he just glared back at me.

Priorities—I've noticed that as a person ages, his priorities change. I have much more interest now in people, philosophy, and the spiritual realm than I did when I was younger. Of course being fortunate enough to have a wife that I have grown to love and appreciate more each day over the past almost forty years, four children that are no doubt far above average, and at last count nine self declared gifted grandchildren contributes to placing family at the top of the list of my priorities. "Things" are not as important to me as they used to be. However, in the "things" category there are some "things" that have become increasingly more important during the past few years. These include a top-of-the-line king-sized bed, a comfortable rocker-recliner chair, a good television set with remote control, and quality toilet paper.

Strange Students—It seems to me that we have more students that could be categorized as "strange" now than we did in the past. It wouldn't surprise me if they are allergic to themselves. They think an apostrophe is something you eat like spaghetti. We talked about purchasing some temporary wash off tattoos for the teachers to put on their bodies so that they would look more like the parents of these kids and so that the kids would feel more comfortable and like they are at home. One of the kids wants to make a wooden coffin in shop class. He had a little smile on his face, that reminded me of a possum, when he told me that he has someone in mind that might need it but he wouldn't say who. He requested that I issue a "restraining order" to some kid that has been bothering him. He said that a judge had issued one to his dad to keep him away from his mom and it worked. His neighbor reported that the kid punted chickens around the yard at home and made a terrible mess. He told me that he was thinking of cutting his ear off. I told him he better not because, although it might help his career as an artist, he could not be a musician because he wouldn't have an "ear for music."

Stormy Petrels—I heard an older person say about a kid, "He has a bad case of the lazys." That really hit the nail on the head. He also described a parent who seems to always be around when things go bad as a stormy petrel. I looked the term up and found out that a stormy petrel is a bird that seems to enjoy turmoil and the foulest of weather and appears when the waves of the sea are the highest. Come to think of it, I know of a lot of people who could fit that definition.

CPR For Those Who Remain in the Trenches

Concepts, Philosophy, and Reflections

Bench Buddies—There are at least several hundred people, mostly older males, from all parts of the world alive today who, for one short 15 to 30 minute period sometime in the past functioned as my "bench buddy." My relationships with these "bench buddies" were close, personal, and very intense, but also very short-lived. The only thing that we had in common was that we shared a bench or seat of some kind while we rested at a shopping mall, park, or department store or rode on the same airplane, bus, or train. Usually, but not always, both of us had a wife or family that would soon meet us and we were just killing time and resting. Our conversation usually started with some cliche about the weather, sports, how old age is catching up with us, and some reference to how things just are not what they used to be in the good old days. Before we would go our separate ways, never to see each other again, we would show pictures of our families and even talk about personal things that we would be embarrassed to talk about to people we must face every day. Each of these "bench buddies" added one drop into my "bucket of happiness" that, over a lifetime, has filled to overflowing. Bench buddies will never fill our need for life-sustaining and deep lifelong relationships that we should all make a point to develop in our church, family, job, and neighborhood. Marriage is definitely not meant to be a "bench buddy" type of relationship. Unfortunately too many modern marriages are just that. While I drink coffee and visit with "bench buddies" to pass the time I like to "people watch." I made up a game called "Miss America." We all know that you can't judge a book by its cover and that prejudice is wrong. We also know the importance of first impressions. Our impression of persons when we first see them is not based on any particular predetermined objective set of criteria. We simply gather together all of our prejudices, biases, preferences, and likes and dislikes and make a quick, on-the-spot subjective evaluation. Some men prefer women who are heavy, have long hair, are tall, and mature. Other guys like thin ladies with short hair. Being in the education profession, I am accustomed to assigning grades to kids. When I play "Miss America," I arbitrarily rate adult women in my mind as they pass my bench using the following scale: (1) sickening (2) very ugly (3) ugly (4) below average (5) average (6) above average (7) pretty (8) beautiful (9) very beautiful (10) Miss America. I make allowances for age and give extra points if the lady is smiling. I gave my wife, Myra, a 10 when she came by to say she was ready to head for home. I know I'm prejudiced when it comes to her. I hope there isn't some old lady sitting on a bench rating men as I walk by. I know how she would rate me.

It would be fun and enlightening to get a bunch of my friends together out at the mall and compare our rating systems. We could all sit down with yellow scratch pads and rate each woman as she emerged from the escalator. The activity could even lead to some higher math as we would need to arrive at an average, mean, and median. A women's auxiliary probably would soon be organized to rate men. National and international organizations would follow. People who judged livestock in 4-H when they were kids would probably dominate the blue ribbons when the activity reached the inevitable competitive stage.

Tar Strips—A "tar strip" is defined as any obstacle that is, or is perceived by others as being very minimal or totally unnoticed but is seen by the individual in question as major in nature.

Background—Eunice is a 93-year-old female who prides herself on attending church services every week in spite of failing health. Her hired nurse helps Eunice out of the car at the curb about 10 yards away from the entrance to the church. Two large male ushers, one on each side of her, help her start walking. Her feet start slowly shuffling with very short steps never leaving the concrete. Her steps gradually speed up and Eunice seems to be making progress. Suddenly she stops. Neither one of the church ushers can see any reason for stopping. Then they notice a tar strip in a crack in the concrete that rises only about a fourth of an inch above the surface. Eunice sees the tar strip as a major obstacle and succeeds in stepping over it only with considerable help from both ushers.

All of us have tar strips in our lives. We perceive some physical, psychological, or social obstacle as major even though others may hardly notice it.

We must be alert to other's tar strips. Some task that seems simple to us could be perceived by another person as impossible and cause enough stress to cause that person to give up hope or even contemplate suicide.

The Inspector—Every morning Myra and I work together to make the bed. We are always sure to puff up the pillows just right and tuck in the sheet down on the bottom end of the bed in a manner that should satisfy even the most particular Navy inspectors that I experienced back in the '50s. I started to wonder why we do that and all of the other "getting ready for inspection" type things. After all, nobody comes into our private bedroom but us. I've come to the conclusion that there resides within each of us an "inspector." In reality we don't need to satisfy anybody but ourselves. Getting ready for company to visit is something else all together. We are even more particular then, but even on those occasions we are our own worst critics. Although sometimes we probably cause ourselves to do things that are not totally necessary, the "inspector" in us does keep us from becoming slobs.

Church Van Trips—Every Wednesday morning Myra and her friend Lou, take the church van full of senior citizens from a retirement apartment on an outing. They usually pick up about a dozen delightful ladies ranging from kids in their seventies to double seniors who are nearing the century mark. Sometimes they go shopping, sometimes out to eat at a restaurant; but wherever they go, they have more fun than a bunch of grade school kids. One of these ladies was bragging that she had recently been elected to serve as vice-president of the residence group. She explained that the position of vice-president in that group is more important than in other groups made up of younger persons. It seems that by the time a resident has lived in the home long enough to accumulate enough friends and political influence to be elected president, she is so old that it is very likely that she will die before her term is over. These gals are survivors— tough as nails yet as kind and gentle as lambs. They give the old Frank Sinatra song "You Make Me Feel So Young" a double meaning. One bought a lifetime supply of toilet paper. Another one said, with a chuckle, that she still enjoys riding on the merry-go-round but she worries all the time she is riding that the horse she is on will be in the up position when she must get off. They appreciate and look forward with great anticipation to little things that most of us take for granted, like eating the first vine-ripened tomato of the season. All of them have been blessed with a tremendous sense of humor, as have Myra and Lou. It is a great combination and everyone really has a great time. Today Lou was on vacation so Myra was driving the van. Luther Place is undergoing remodeling and enlarging so the drive that leads to the front door has been torn up. That made it necessary for Myra to do some difficult backing of the van quite a distance to the front door when she delivered the group back after shopping. They were all quiet as church mice while she was backing the van. When the job was successfully completed, they clapped and cheered loudly and congratulated Myra like she had won some event in the Olympics. Myra got out of the van and responded with a sweeping bow. I wish I had been there!

"Detroit Syndrome"—Detroit, Michigan is known as the new car capital of the world. The idea promoted by this industry is that this year's model is better than last year's model. New, young, and up-to-date cars are to be sought after. Older cars have served their purpose and are ready for the junk yard. If a car survives for 50 years, it is declared an antique and not functional, not useful, but blocked up and put into a museum.

The "Detroit Syndrome," in human relations terms, places great value on "newness." Young persons are sought out. Older persons are discarded. More emphasis is placed on creative new ideas than on the wisdom that comes from experience. We have far too many antique teachers and administrators around who have allowed themselves to be blocked up and put into a museum. Antique teachers may be tarnished and scarred, but they should be respected and valued highly.

Some psychologists have characterized our modern culture as a "throw away society." Many materials are built to be used for a short time and then thrown away—i.e. razors, wrapping paper, new cars every two years, and a new marriage partner or job whenever we feel the urge.

We need just the opposite philosophy if we expect to develop any stability whatsoever. We need quality, long-lasting relationships. We need roots and traditions. We need people who will stay at the same job long enough to develop deep relationships. You can't delegate relationships. We need educators in our schools who have been around long enough to provide "institutional memory." A new broom may sweep clean but an old broom knows where to sweep.

Stray Dogs and Have Not Kids—If you pet a stray dog, you have made a friend for life. Stray dogs are not accustomed to getting attention and kindness. When they do receive attention and kindness, they respond more intensely than well accepted, cute, family pets do. Sometimes the excitement leads to jumping all over the person who befriended them. That person may have a hard time getting the dog to accept that he can't spend all of his time with it.

In the same way, if you befriend a "have not kid," you have made a friend for life. These kids are not accustomed to attention and kindness. When these children do receive attention and kindness, they respond more intensely than well accepted, cute, popular kids do. Sometimes the excitement of these kids leads to wanting to be constantly in the presence of the person who befriended them. You might have a hard time getting these kids to accept the fact that you can't spend all of your time with them.

One little mentally handicapped girl made a mirror in art class to give to her mom on Mother's Day. The mirror had "MOM" and a heart etched on it. When she showed it to me she held it upside down and I thought it had "WOW" written on it. I just read the "WOW" and she was very happy because she thought I really liked it. When I realized that I had goofed, it wasn't even necessary to tell her. She was happy.

Every day I eat lunch with a kid who is severely mentally and physically handicapped. He is a real joy to be around and honest to the core. He says things to me, the principal, that need to be said but other kids are afraid to say. One day when I quietly passed some gas, he told me, "Something stinks around here and I think it is you." He pinched me when I didn't wear green on St. Patrick's Day. I had it coming but other kids wouldn't think of pinching the principal. We have a daily ritual that seems to make us psychologically closer than any two people who are not married could possibly be—sort of a "the two of you shall become one" consummation of the marriage vows type of ritual. When we both are done eating, we stack our trays and dishes together (like we are merging our souls), and he carries them over to the garbage and dishwashing area for both of us. He has a fit if I miss lunch for some reason. We all would be better off if we had more friends like that. We are good for each other. When our staff and his parents met to develop his Individual Educational Plan (IEP) we all agreed that it would be a good learning experience for him to work some each day with the building custodian. We assigned him the responsibility of sweeping the hallways each day immediately after lunch at 12:30 p.m. We had the custodian give him extensive training on the proper way to carry out this duty. His teacher taught him how to look at the clock and know when it was 12:30 p.m. You could set your clock by when he was out in the hallway cheerfully and proudly contributing to the cleanliness of "his" school. One day we had a Parent-Teacher meeting at 12:30 p.m. and the hall was crowded with those attending the meeting. My buddy came along with his broom and politely demanded that all of these adults move so he could carry out his sweeping responsibility. He was very dependable but not too flexible. I am sure that in the future he will be gainfully employed and a contributing citizen in "his" community.

Get Things Done—We buried a good friend today. He was only one year older than me. We all thought that he was in great physical condition. Just last summer he had filled in on the church slow-pitch softball team when some of the younger guys didn't show up. And he usually got a hit too! He just had a stroke and died. After an initial period of feeling shock and grief, I realized that the clock was ticking and that my friend's death should be a wake-up call for everyone to live life to its fullest each and every day.

I must quit just thinking and planning. I must DO. I must get things done. I MUST—get my memories recorded on paper—write and read poetry—hold newborn babies—attend music concerts—live it up at athletic contests and auctions—walk through the woods holding hands with my wife—take the time to visit with friends and family—go fishing instead of talk about fishing—sing old familiar hymns with gusto—enjoy productive hours at the museum and library—attend country-music shows, folk music and arts festivals, circuses, and parades—bask in the glorious atmosphere of college basketball games instead of just reading about the excitement the next day in the newspaper—experience the unique beauty of each of the National Parks and the feel and smell of each of the major league baseball stadiums—go to places that I have only read about—marvel at the majesty of the stars at night and focus on the beauty of cloud formations in the daytime—publicly and vigorously protest social injustice instead of wishing years later that I had done so—pray hard and often—tell my family and friends that I love them—feel, with greater intensity, the presence of God's grace in my life and the excitement of celebrating Holy Communion.

I'M GOING TO move toward the noise, the excitement, and the action not away from it—make ALL of my time "quality time"—plant trees and flowers, laugh often and loud, enjoy my grandkids, and visit my shut-in friends. All of these things have taken on an urgency that I never felt when I was younger.

When I am on my death-bed, I don't want to look back on my life and wish I had done things that I could have done during my life but had not done. I'm going to try to do all the things I might some day wish I had done while I am still able to do them.

I'm going to BE AWARE, FOCUS, APPRECIATE, FEEL, EXPERIENCE, and DO. I'm going to get things done—NOW—before it is too late!

The Ezekiel Expectation—The story in the Bible about Ezekiel goes something like this—Ezekiel found himself in a valley covered with lots of very dry bones. The Lord told him to bring those dry bones to life, and through faith, he did. He was told that the people of Israel were like those dry bones without any hope. The same thing could be done for them.

Many of the critics of education are expecting schools to make the same miracle happen. That is, to take a hopeless situation and breathe life into it. All educators face this "Ezekiel Expectation" but those most often afflicted by it are special education teachers and coaches. The amazing thing is that educators usually come through! The profession is filled with Ezekiels.

The "Nazareth Concept"—The Bible tells us that Nazareth was the hometown of Jesus. The residents of the town undoubtedly knew him quite well, yet they were among the last to recognize that he was the great person that he was. They reasoned that "nothing great could come out of Nazareth" and that all great persons come from someplace else far away.

We have that same idea, the Nazareth Concept, in operation today. It seems that all of the real experts come from places at least two days' driving time from where we live. The programs that they promote sound great and we would like to observe them in operation, but we can't go that far from home just to visit one program. I know a lady who teaches in a city in California where one of these really great programs that we heard about is in operation. I asked her about it, and she hadn't even heard of it. She asked me to tell her more about the great program that she had heard about in a town in Kansas just a few miles from where I live. I hadn't heard of it.

Many Kansas school districts look for new superintendents and football coaches (seemingly the two most important positions in any school district) in places like California and Maine. Most of our people have to travel long distances in order to be considered an expert.

The "Jericho Problem Solving Process" —We have all heard the story of how Joshua fought the battle of Jericho. He and his followers marched around the city many times over a period of many days, making lots of noise, and "the walls came tumbling down." The same type of process often works when a group of people are attempting to come to agreement on an issue where it seems like no consensus can possibly be reached. The secret is to march around and around the issue over a long period of time, making lots of noise and "the walls will come tumbling down." This could be called the "Jericho Problem Solving Process."

The "Watergate Lesson" —We should learn from history. Persons who make mistakes the first time have an excuse. They don't know any better. Those who make the same mistake a second time are just plain stupid.

One of the major lessons that all of us should have learned from the Watergate Incidents of the 1970s is that those persons who worked for the President during that period of time did not serve the President's best interest by insulating him from his critics and always agreeing with him even though they knew that he was headed for trouble unless he changed his tactics. President Nixon's advisors were in awe of his power and therefore, instead of disagreeing with him when they knew that he was wrong, functioned only as "Yes, Men" and "Nodders." The President was out of touch with the people. He needed to have his advisors tell him what he needed to hear not what he wanted to hear. If they had only spoken up, they could have prevented one of the worst scandals in our history from happening. At the time they felt that they were serving the President by blindly agreeing with, supporting, and promoting whatever the President thought. Just the opposite was true. The President needed those who cared about him to put him in touch with reality rather than to blindly follow him.

School administrators need the same thing. They don't need "Yes, Men" or "Nodders," they need "Booger Men"—colleagues who have the character and care enough about them to tell them when they have a "booger on their shirt collar" or "egg on their face." Teachers and assistant principals are usually closer to the students and parents than principals are. They know things that principals need to know. They should be made aware that principals not only will tolerate their disagreement on occasion but expect and appreciate it. William Wrigley Jr. said, "When two men in a business always agree, one of them is unnecessary."

Sometimes the Best Thing to Do is Nothing. Most problems (things that are not okay) need to have some action taken to remedy the condition. On the other hand, there are some types of problems that will tend to take care of themselves if just left alone. Sometimes it is best to do nothing, but exercise patience. Some examples are listed here:

1. The snow that falls on your driveway will melt eventually if left alone. Piling it up next to the driveway in your yard will cause little dirty piles of snow to remain far after most of the snow has melted. I have found that some less thoughtful persons accuse those of us that engage in this practice of being lazy. These people can be written off as just jealous.

2. After a shower or bath your body will dry without the use of a towel if you are just patient and give it a little time. You can always do other things like brush your teeth, comb your hair, or shave while you naturally dry off. If you are in a big hurry, you can jump up and down to speed the process. One of the things that causes people to get ulcers is being in too big of a hurry all the time. By drying off naturally, you won't get ulcers and also will save a lot of money by not having to wash so many towels. It is a good idea to have a few towels on hand for visitors as they might not be as enlightened as you are.

3. Sores and scabs heal best without attention. Just keep them covered and leave them alone and allow them to heal. This is even more true with "figurative" scabs. Human relationships that are a bit uneasy heal best if you "don't pick the scab." It's not the itch that does the most permanent damage but real injury is caused by scratching the itch. Most often we are most seriously damaged not by what happens to us, but by how we handle what happens to us. It has been said that our success and happiness in life depends 10 percent on what happens to us and 90 percent on how we react to it.

4. Things that you can't do anything about or choose not to do anything about are best not talked about.

5. Sometimes action is called for. Sometimes it is much wiser not to act. Knowing the difference comes from experience and maturity.

We had a television set that just quit working. Myra told me to take it in to the certified repair place in town but I knew that if I did that, they would charge me a fortune just to look at it and they wouldn't even do that until they were ready to. I knew of a little repair shop that was operated by an old man where we used to take radios to get them fixed. I took the chance that the old man was still in business and would look at my TV for free and fix it for little or nothing if it could be fixed . The old man was happy to see me and had his grandson help me carry the TV set into his small shop. The shop was a mess—not at all like I had remembered it and I had a few misgivings. It was too late then to change my mind so I left my TV set there and told my old friend that I would check with him later in the day. Ole and I were having coffee that afternoon and I asked him to go with me to check on my TV. When we went into the old man's shop, he was still sitting where he had been sitting that morning and apologized for not looking at my TV. He said that his grandson had left and he couldn't walk by himself. I thanked him for his good intentions and since it was too late by that time to take it any place else, I took it back home. I plugged it in and it worked just fine. Since that time it has stopped working several times, but a good whack on the side fixes it. Sometimes you only need to do a little, not much, to resolve a situation .

It Takes No Brains To Get Mad—This morning I cut some brush out from around the shed in our backyard. I felt something on my head and thought that it was a branch from a tree. When I reached up to knock the branch away I felt a sharp stabbing pain on the top of my head. A wasp had stung me! Fortunately, I needed a haircut at the time and he didn't get his stinger completely into my skin. He was mad at me for disturbing his nest and just kept flying at me. I ran backward toward the house, swatting my sickle at him. I have never witnessed such anger in my life. He just kept diving at me! Later, when I had time to reflect on the incident, I thought it was a great example of the fact that it takes hardly any brains at all to get all mad and angry. That wasp's brain couldn't have been larger than the head of a pin. When people show that same type of angry behavior, I now think about the wasp and realize how little of the brain that person must be using.

Both Shoes and People Wear Out From The Top Down—Back in the 1940s shoes wore out on the bottom first and later on the top. It was not uncommon to see people with holes in the bottom of their shoes. When this happened we took our shoes to a shoe repairman and he resoled them. People were that way too; they worked physically so hard that their bottoms (their bodies) wore out before their tops (their minds), and they died.

Now it is a rare thing to see holes in the bottom of a pair of shoes. Today we throw shoes away either because their tops wear out or because they are out of fashion. We benefit so much from all of the modern technology that most people's bodies (their bottoms) survive longer than their minds (tops). Rest homes are full of these poor old people. Too bad you can't re-soul a worn out mind.

Goodwill Accounts—Everybody knows that they are in trouble when they receive a notice from the bank showing that they have spent more money than they have put in. Our financial bank account must balance. I have preached to kids for years that the same thing is true in regard to each of our "goodwill accounts." I have made it a practice to call kids who do well in school into my office and congratulate them and tell them that I would be honored if some day they included my name on a list of references. Then I go on to tell them that a good way to live their life is to look upon it as an opportunity to accumulate as many persons as possible who they could call on to write a reference for them some day when they might need it. In other words, live your life in such a manner that you keep a healthy balance on the plus side in your goodwill account.

During my high school, college, and Navy years, I didn't have a car so I either hitch-hiked or walked almost everywhere I went. At that time I really appreciated the goodwill of those kind souls who gave me a free ride. I vowed that some day, when I was "rich enough to own a car," I would return the favor by never passing up an opportunity to pick up a hitch-hiker. I knew that I had a negative balance in my goodwill account, but I was confident that I would even things up in the future. I looked forward to that time. When I got my first car, I would drive out of my way to pick up hitch-hikers. Then times changed. No matter how much a person would like to help, it became a very dangerous practice to pick up hitch-hikers. On those occasions that I do stop to offer some pedestrian a ride, I have been told "No thanks, I'm walking for exercise." Now I'm stuck with a negative balance in my goodwill account and feel the need to even things up. I was blessed as a kid to have been the recipient of a flood of goodwill from family, neighbors, teachers, and church members. This was great then, and I am glad I was so fortunate, but it has added to my goodwill account imbalance. This is great motivation to get busy paying back! I only hope I live long enough to come close to balancing out my goodwill account. I'll continue to look for disabled cars along the highway and do what I can to help those who need help. Little do the recipients of my goodwill know that they are helping me repay a long standing debt.

The Hate Vacuum—The Cold War is over. The Berlin Wall has been torn down. Now we can live in a world full of peace, love, and brotherhood. Not so! There seems to be a large group of people who just can't seem to be happy unless they have someone to distrust, hate, and feel is conspiring against them. These people come from all across the political spectrum and from all racial groups and religious persuasions. Now that they don't have the Communists to worry about, they have taken to distrusting each other. They are sure that they are right and that anyone who disagrees with them is wrong. They know that those who are wrong are meeting someplace and planning a conspiracy to get them. These paranoids claim to know that the government has a "tornado making machine" and is using it to punish the Mid-West for some unknown reason. They polarize every issue. There is no middle ground, only extremes.

During the decade of the 1940s, when I developed most of my belief system progressing from age six to sixteen, our nation was engaged in World War II. All Americans had a common enemy, the Nazis and Japanese, to pull us together. We admired our military heroes, policemen, and teachers. Now that we don't have a real common enemy, the rednecks feel a "hate vacuum," and seem to feel the need to create an enemy.

Many of these distrustful souls have taken to bashing the closest person in authority. Most often that happens to be local teachers and school administrators, government officials, and policeman. The very people who were most admired years ago have now become the villain that it is in style to criticize, belittle, and bash.

I guess that we can take some comfort from the fact that the basketball playoffs will soon begin and much of this anger and general negative way at looking at life will be diverted to those poor souls who serve as basketball referees.

Don't Get Mad—Simple advice is usually the best advice. Quite often we are so close to a situation that we can't see the obvious. I started to tell Ole about the details of why I was getting upset. He said, "Before you get too far, let me tell you what I think you should do about it." I couldn't see how he could know the solution to my dilemma before he even knew anything about it, but because I respect his opinion, I asked him to go on talking. He said that the best advice that he could give me was, "Don't get mad. It's not in your best interest." I was surprised to hear him say that. I had every right in the world to get mad. After all, in my opinion I had been wronged.

Ole went on to explain his rationale. If you get mad, it hurts you more than the guy that you get mad at. Mad leads to negative outlook, which leads to anger, which leads to bitterness, which leads to alienation. Nobody wants to be around a guy that is mad, negative, angry, bitter and alienated. Be a little selfish and look out for your own best interests. Don't get mad. It's not in your own best interest. Simple but true!

Weekly Gatherings—Church Attendance and High School Athletics—A community is defined in the dictionary as "a group of people living together as a social unit and having interests in common." Attending church services together and supporting the same high school athletic team are two very similar common interests that draw people together as a community on a weekly basis. Both of these have a strong emotional element and work toward creation of the spirit of "we." A casual observer will notice that week after week, both in church and in the bleachers, individuals tend to sit in the same general location in relation to the group to which they belong . This consistency of behavior gives them feelings of stability and belonging. Both groups exist over a period of years and a very close relationship tends to develop between individuals. When one lists his best friends, he usually begins by listing those with whom he works daily and worships regularly with, and associates with weekly at high school athletic events. Of course the objectives of high school primarily consider the effect of those participating. It is also true, however, that many other persons benefit from high school athletics. This is nothing to be unhappy about. As a matter of fact, it is a very positive result.

Itches and Cures—I have noticed that whatever causes an itch is high profile and big news but whatever cures an itch is soon forgotten. It may sound trite to those unfortunate persons who have ongoing battles with alcoholism, cancer, or abuse; but I have fought a lifelong battle with athlete's foot. I have tried dozens of remedies, some of these work better than others, but like an alcoholic, I always will consider myself a recovering athlete's foot victim rather than a winner in the battle against it. When the itch is present, it gets much of my attention. When symptoms do not exist, I don't really appreciate that fact and give credit due to whatever medicine stopped the itch. We never seem to appreciate all of the diseases and other negative things that we don't experience. Just think of how much we don't suffer from for which we have reason to be thankful. Running schools is the same. When trouble exists, we all notice it, and it gets much attention. We never seem to appreciate it as much as we should when things run smoothly and everyone is happy. We all have a tendency to take good for granted. Cures should get as much attention and be just as big news as itches.

Doorknobs—The doorknob can be seen as a symbol of power and control. A door that has a knob on it can be opened, shut, or locked. If a door has no knob, you have no control over it and the door becomes just like part of the wall.

private office. At birth, and all through infancy, the knob on the door leading to this private space is on the outside. The infant does not control access to his "private space"—others come and go at will.

The process of maturation should involve a gradual ability of the individual to change the doorknob leading to his private space from the outside to the inside. By having the doorknob on the inside, where his "self" resides, the individual gains control of the door. He can control who comes through the door. He decides if and when to become angry and whether negative influences get to him. He is in charge of his own life. He has power.

If you look carefully at the famous picture, "Christ at the Door Knocking," you will notice that there is no knob on the outside of the door. The message of the picture is that, because the doorknob is on the inside, it is controlled by the person Christ is seeking. We were given the responsibility of making the decision whether or not to allow Christ access to our lives.

It is a sign of maturity to be in control of our own lives by having our doorknob on our side of the door. This is also a tremendous responsibility that we assume. We can no longer blame what happens to us on others.

No one should be totally vulnerable. Therefore, it is necessary for us to decide when to shut our door. On the other hand, no one should be totally isolated and alone. Therefore, we must keep our door open enough to develop relationships. We can choose to use our doors either constructively or destructively. Because we have chosen to have the doorknob on our side of the door, we control our own destiny. Too many people don't make that choice.

Finding Myra Jane—Today is my wedding anniversary. I let Myra choose how we would celebrate. I let her choose between going to the middle school band concert or attending the Board of Education meeting.

When I was a senior in college, I learned to drive a car. I noticed that when I pulled into a parking lot, I had two choices. I could take the first open space and then possibly discover that a better space was available, or I could pass up several good spaces only to find that there were no better spaces available. At the time, I thought that choosing a parking spot must be much like choosing a wife. I had passed up several good possibilities with the hope that I might find someone better later. As a senior I started to wonder whether there was really anyone better. Maybe I had been too picky and should have settled for one of those that I had passed up.

Then I met Myra Jane Shoreen. I saw her standing in the lunch line in the college cafeteria. I knew right away that she was what I had been waiting for. Other girls had been like common cars. Myra was a Cadillac (Swedish variety). She was the pick of the litter. She had pedigree, class, charisma, physical beauty, brains, and all that anyone could ever ask for. But would she even consider me? I was a second year senior so I only had the rest of that semester to gain her favor. My future happiness was ensured when she agreed to date me and finally gave her consent to marry me in the near future. I got two things from Bethany College—an education and a wife. The more important was Myra Jane.

Rainbow Girls—If I didn't have four great kids and nine far above average grandkids, I would miss much of the beauty that exists in the world. There would be no one to call me on the phone and say, "Dad, there is a full rainbow on the east horizon, you better go outside and see it!" I call my three daughters my "Rainbow Girls." On those days that I only see the clouds and rain, they see rainbows and the promise of budding flowers. The world needs more "Rainbow Girl" types to point out hope and beauty to those who see only gray skies.

A Guy Needs A Wife—I just can't imagine how a guy could get along if he weren't married. How would he know where to park when he enters a parking lot or how to find his car when it is time to go home? I would never know when to turn on the windshield wipers if Myra weren't there to tell me although it must rain harder and sooner on the passenger side than on the driver's side. She also is usually of the opinion that I should speed up, making me believe that the car goes faster on my side than on hers. It would seem to me that it would be worth getting married if only to have someone to help make the king-sized bed in the morning. The only time we don't make our bed is when we are on vacation, and then we don't make it only because the maid would get mad if we took the pleasure away from her. I don't mean that not being married would be like being on vacation because you wouldn't make your bed. Not at all! In my opinion a guy needs a wife as much as he needs pockets. When my garage door opener quit working last year, I relied on Myra to jump out of the truck when we pulled into the driveway and open the garage door. Some people refer to their car by some cute name, like Lizzy or Rueben. I joked that my garage opener's name was Myra. I told the kids, "There's nothing wrong with my garage door opener. She's in great shape." Myra good-naturedly countered that in the middle of the winter, when it was really cold, the name of the garage door opener would be Duane (my middle name). I got it fixed.

Everybody Needs A Grandma—No matter how old we get, we

all need a grandma! I have observed first-hand how great my grandkids get treated by their grandmas and I have come to the conclusion that the older a guy gets, the more he needs a grandma. Oh to be so kissed, hugged, cuddled, coddled, and in other ways overindulged! When we get older, we experience more abuse, criticism, and negative comments than we did as infants when we had the benefit of our grandma's unique and unqualified acceptance. There is no doubt but that infants need and appreciate being "grandma-ed." It wouldn't be right to take that away from babies and give it to old men, but it would be nice if both groups could experience it. Men get grandma-ed by their wives, but that is inherently a different relationship. There is an element of equality that exists in the husband-wife relationship. A man's feeling toward his grandma hasn't even a trace of equality in it. He looks up to her as kind of a godlike creature and she looks at him as a perfect gift of God that is of unequaled value and treats him as such. It's too bad that grandmas can't live forever. Everyone needs a Grandma Sody or Grandma Maxine to hug and kiss them, carry them upstairs, and tuck them in bed one more time.

STLT—Some things that happen are so emotionally overwhelming that they cause a person to experience the Shiver, Tears, and Lump in the Throat so you can't talk condition, better known as "STLT." Macho type grown men who pride themselves in being tough and laid-back always attempt to avoid letting anyone else around them know that they could be so affected. They fake pseudo-bugs in their eyes and suddenly for no reason experience coughing spells to avoid detection. It seems that everyone has a different set of events that will trigger the STLT reaction. A person's background and the significant events in our unique personal histories cause us to be different. In my case the following will do it every time:

(1)   The American flag carried by marching military personnel leading a parade.
(2)   Singing "Children of the Heavenly Father" or "A Mighty Fortress is Our God."
(3)   Looking at a newborn child—especially if it is my own child or grandchild.
(4)   When any marching band comes by in a parade.
(5)   When the Messiah choir sings the "Hallelujah Chorus."
(6   Three times on December 24th: (a) At about 5:30 p.m. when I look out of the window at the falling snow and flashback all of the Christmas Eves of the past and think of what is going to happen this night, (b) When the entire family is settled around the supper table and it is time to say grace, and (c) At the midnight church service

when we all hold candles and the choir and congregation sing "All Hail to Thee, Oh Blessed Morn!"

The STLT condition can hit any one of us at any time. We might be watching television, listening to the radio, reading, or just talking to others when something triggers it. Defining what triggers our STLT condition probably defines us as individuals and describes how each of us differs from one another.

I Want To Stay Eight Forever—Last night I relaxed by listening to some of my favorite music. The Frank Sinatra song, "That Was a Very Good Year" started me thinking about my own life and which years could be called "very good" years. Myra and I had a deep discussion about which decade we each thought was the best decade. At first I picked the 1940s but changed my mind when I remembered World War II, that my dad had died and we had very little worldly goods, and that Myra and my kids and grandkids were not a part of my life then. Myra said that she remembered wishing when she was eight years old that she would stay eight forever. After thinking about it for a while, I remembered that I was also totally content at age eight. I asked several of the staff members which decade they would pick as their best decade and if they were happy when they were eight years old. They had fun with the exercise but I sensed that a couple of them wondered what I was up to and felt that there must be something sinister behind my question. My buddy Harold Hubble told about an incident he will never forget that happened to him when he was just a young kid growing up in a small town in Nebraska. WWII dominated everything at the time even the games kids played. Harold was out in his yard playing by himself, pretending that he was a hero in the war with bombs dropping all around him. He threw an old metal license plate up into the air as high as he could and then ran, with his head down, as the "bomb" would land close to him. The license plate hit him directly on top of his head. He wasn't such a hero when his mom took him to get stitches in the cut. Harold was embarrassed when his mother tried to explain how her son could get hit on the head by a license plate. Harold also remembers that he bought cough drops instead of candy at the movie because he got more for his money and they lasted longer.

The Crumb Company—In the Navy they had what was called the "Crumb Company" for guys who didn't keep up with the rest of us or caused trouble. They were not moving toward graduation from Boot Camp but just marking time: practicing marching, washing clothes, drilling, and standing one inspection after another. They were the outcasts of Boot Camp and were treated with disgust and disrespect by everyone. I wish we could start a middle school Crumb Company! I know it would not be allowed. I bet it would work though.

Holy Cities, Parades, and Yearbook Pictures—If you stop to think of it, all of us have what to us is a "Holy City." To car racing enthusiasts it might be Indianapolis; to a professional football fan it could be Green Bay; to Jews it is Jerusalem. Moslems were taught by their leader, Mohammed, that one of the five duties of their faith is to make a pilgrimage to the holy city of Mecca. They face Mecca and pray five times a day. To those of us of Swedish ancestry in Kansas, the city of Lindsborg is our Holy City. Most modern day Swedes don't face Lindsborg when they pray; they are much too liberated for that. But we do feel an obligation to "pilgrimage" to the Holy City three times a year—every summer for Midsummers Festival, every fall for homecoming or Hylingsfest, and every Holy Week for the Messiah Festival.

We usually go to Lindsborg on the interstate highway. This time we decided to take our time and really experience the beauty of Kansas by driving on less traveled local roads. As we approached the small town of Gypsum, Kansas, we read the following message on a neatly painted sign, "Gypsum next 13 exits" (driveways), and another sign that said, "Emergency Snow Route" (of course it was the only route).

Last fall when we were watching the Hylingsfest parade, it seemed to me that the parade was just going around and around the block. It was almost as if I was seeing the same Grade School and High School bands, Shriners on their tiny motor scooters, cars carrying the mayors of small Kansas towns, scout troops, 4-H clubs, kennel clubs with their dogs on lease (and several stray mongrel dogs who joined the procession on their own), Grange members marching proudly, retirement home residents in buses, clowns, old cars, new cars, National Guard bands, tractors, fire engines from every township in Kansas, and even cement trucks. I wondered if we might be witnessing the first eternal parade. Now I know why I am always asked to speak last at administrator meetings. It's for the same reason that the horses come last in the parade; they leave such a mess that nobody wants to come after them. One year it rained on parade day. That didn't seem to matter. We're talking about the real heroes of Mid-America, and they were not going to let a little rain stop them. Witnessing dedication like that brought tears to my eyes!

Yesterday was Easter so quite naturally we spent the day in Lindsborg. I was looking through the printed program for the Messiah and noticed that the pictures of the soloists showed young and attractive persons. I noted that the pictures only slightly resembled the real persons when they got up to sing. The real persons were much older, heavier, and no where near as attractive. I remember trying this trick myself a few years ago. I gave the yearbook staff a picture of me that had been taken back in 1955 to be put in the yearbook above my name on the administration page. The Messiah soloists can get by with doing this because they are far away from most of the crowd and many people don't see them because they listen to them over the radio. It certainly didn't work for me. I guess the flat-top haircut gave it away.

We usually forget to send for tickets to the Messiah until all of the good seats are taken and have to settle for seats in the front row where we can't see the chorus. Our seats are only a few feet from the soloists so I try to get some kind of response from them by giving them a thumbs up, wink, and smile. They don't seem to see any humor in it.

Keep Moving—The water faucet in the bathroom has been dripping a little for the last several weeks. It worries me that our water bill will be higher than it should be, but the cut-off valve in the basement doesn't work and it has been so cold outside lately that I hate to go outside and dig under the snow to open the manhole lid to turn off the water so I can fix it. Rather than admit that I'm lazy and not much of a plumber, I have tried to convince myself that smart people purposely keep the water in the pipes in their homes moving during cold weather so it doesn't freeze. Come to think of it, that same concept is true when it comes to people; we need to keep moving and active or we will have a tendency to freeze up and become cold and dysfunctional. Rust will also form and clog things up when water in pipes doesn't move to carry it away. We can be the victim of rust ourselves if we are physically, mentally, or psychologically idle too long. We can't stop the rust from forming but if we keep active, we can prevent it from building up and affecting our efficiency. Maybe our biggest enemy is complacency. At least when we are a little bit uncomfortable and have unmet needs, we are motivated to move and be active. Old age probably won't hurt us so much as the inactivity of body and mind if we allow "that old rocking chair" to get us. Use it or lose it. Keep moving!

Beautiful People Are Right Under Our Noses—We went to the granddaughter's dance recital last night. There were about 200 kids who performed two numbers each. In the past I made fun of persons who wore a T-shirt that said "I survived" something on it but when we finally walked out of the recital I would have proudly purchased one that said, "I survived the dance recital." Of course, none of the other kids even came close to matching my grandkids, but one of the older more talented young ladies was so great I caught myself saying to myself, "What is a tremendous girl like that doing in Topeka? She ought to be in New York or Hollywood." Then I looked around and realized that neither of those places have anything that can compare to the wonderful people we have in Topeka.

And I bet thousands of other small towns all across America feel that same type of pride. A small town near to Topeka can boast that the world champion horseshoe pitcher lives there. I may be a little prejudiced, but I feel that the most beautiful people in the world live in Topeka, Kansas. If we knew of a better place to live, we would have moved there long ago. Talent and beauty are right under our noses every day. We only need to wake up and recognize it when we see it.

Social Recognition—In Kansas, especially if you work in a school, you are expected to look everyone you meet straight in the eye, and say, "Hi," to them even if you aren't sure if you know them. It is like culture shock to go out of state to a big city and experience the "I don't even know that you exist" attitude when you meet people on the street and on elevators. At first they seem startled when we talk to them, but usually after a while it is evident that they have been thirsting for recognition and really appreciate it.

Coloring Inside of the Lines—Back when I was a kid, we were told that we should stay inside the lines when we did art work with crayons in a coloring book. It was no big deal if we made a mistake and got outside of the lines, but if we did, we knew that we had made a mistake. We tried to stay inside the lines. Why would they have lines if it were not best to color inside of them? That was the idea of the activity and we tried, as best we could, to do it. Then along came some well meaning psychologists who worried that trying to stay inside of the lines stifled creativity and caused kids to feel guilty. It became old fashioned to expect kids to "color inside of the lines." This movement, of course, had much broader ramifications. It became okay to question and violate any and all boundaries of expectation placed on the individual by "repressive authorities." The words "conformity" and "obey" became dirty words, not used by informed persons. A posted speed limit of 55 m.p.h. meant it is okay to drive at 60 m.p.h. The line that separates right from wrong and good from bad became fuzzy. Sick leave is used for purposes other than staying home when a worker is sick so often that employers are agreeing to sick leave payback schemes. Not getting sick should be reward enough. Honest workers should not be rewarded for going to work sick and spreading germs around. But that assumes honesty. Rules, laws, and respect for authority are out and the "It's-okay-to-color-outside-the-lines" philosophy, with an emphasis on tolerance and flexibility, is in. It is incomprehensible to some people that an arbitrary time could be set for events to begin and if a person arrives after that time, he is late and must suffer a consequence. It is as if the words "tardy" and "responsibility" are a foreign language. Is it any wonder that school principals have a difficult time convincing kids that what they that school principals have a difficult time convincing kids that what they say is what they mean? What is wrong with feeling guilt and shame when we do something that is wrong? Isn't it necessary to admit fault and that we made a mistake in order to take the next step which is correction? Just as agreeing to rules and following them is necessary in athletic contests, so do we need conformity in order to form functional communities. Research done by Dr. Stanley Coppersmith, Ph.D., a psychology professor at the University of California, Davis, confirmed the old-fashioned belief that the clearer the rules the parents set, and the more consistently the rules are enforced, the higher a child's self-esteem. The more freedom the child had, on the other hand, the lower his self esteem. One of the origins of self-esteem is in firm and consistent discipline. You generally get what you expect out of children. Let's get back to expecting "coloring inside of the lines" and arriving on time. This expectation is not in conflict with an understanding that each and every human being is singularly unique and that the very nature of the concept of individuality means that no two persons are exactly alike. All of us have a need for creativity and self expression but we also need a clear structure in which to work.

Time—Time seems to be the only thing that everyone in the world can agree on. The time of day is always different in each of the 24 time zones but the system is at least agreed upon by all. Why can't nations agree on other more important things in the same manner?

In the Navy, if I wasn't 15 minutes early, I was considered late. Of course I have not observed it directly, but people tell me that clocks in bars are always set 15 minutes early—not because they are run by Navy people, but because they must have all of the bar customers out of the bar at closing time and that gives the employees an extra 15 minutes to work with. Some of us interpret time literally and put a high premium on punctuality. Others look at time in a more general sense and add the suffix "ish" when they discuss time. The same teacher who gets extremely angry when a student is late to class sees nothing wrong with walking into staff meetings late. Even the time of day seems to be subjective rather than objective.

Childhood diseases and problems experienced during childhood are blessings—All kind people feel sadness and suffer when they witness a child who is ill. We would all like to be able to wave a magic wand and eliminate all of the stress that children face in the process of growing to adulthood. We tend to forget that many of the diseases that children experience cause immunity from that same disease when the child becomes an adult. In that sense it is a blessing to suffer the milder version of a disease as a child rather than the much more severe version of the same disease as an adult. In the same way, children who learn to solve problems as children have a huge advantage over children who have been sheltered from problems as they grow up. We all know that muscles need exercise to develop strength. In the same way, children need to experience a reasonable amount of stress in order to develop character and become successful adults. It is better to experience some problems and temptations as a youth and learn how to deal with them than to suddenly be thrown out in the world as an adult, when we must leave the protection provided by parents, and not be adequately prepared to face the evils of the world. Unfortunately, unlike childhood diseases, it is impossible to immunize children against problems and stress.

Lost? No Way—Last year when Myra and I were driving back to Topeka from our vacation in the Ozarks, we decided to go a new way and got lost. We knew generally where we were, so we convinced ourselves that we weren't really lost and that all we needed to do was to keep going west or north and we would be all right. Anyway, we reasoned, we were on vacation and we should drive slow and see lots of different things so we would enjoy ourselves longer and more. Maybe there are some lessons to be learned from that experience. You must go through life slow enough to enjoy it. If you know generally where you are, and know what direction you must go to get where you should get, and you keep going that direction, you will be okay. A compass is essential. Our conscience could be considered our compass in the area of continuing to go the right moral direction.

Seven Wonders Of The World—As a kid growing up on the plains of Eastern Kansas during the '30s and '40s, my perception of the "Seven Wonders of the World" was different than those listed in the encyclopedia. My list included: (1) Mountains (2) The Ocean (3) Palm Trees (4) Floating in the Great Salt Lake (5) Flying in an airplane (6) Driving a car and (7) The female body. All of these things were unaccessible, remote, far-away, exotic, or forbidden and took on an aura of wonder, and awe. I had read about them but had not experienced them. I learned to drive a car during my senior year of college and first saw mountains and palm trees and experienced swimming in the ocean when I was drafted and traveled by train to California. My family reluctantly experienced floating in the Great Salt Lake every time we drove to California. I first flew in an airplane when I went to Houston, Texas, to attend a meeting for principals. No matter how old I get, all of these continue to be wonders.

Super Myra—The neighbors called to see if Myra was okay. They were worried that she must be sick or something. We had spring break so I was off work for a whole week. I got so bored that I did something that I very rarely do. I mowed the grass. When the neighbors saw me working in the yard, they knew that something must be wrong with Myra. They have grown accustomed to watching her do all of the work around our house and seeing me sitting in a lawn chair "supervising." They were relieved to learn that this had been just a brief and temporary break from normal. Myra is just fine, and things have returned to normal.

When Myra digs small holes in the dirt in the flower garden with her hands and places plants into the ground, her hands get all dirty. She holds her hands out like a doctor about to do surgery—only for a different reason. Doctors hold their hands out after washing them in preparation for doing surgery so they won't get dirty by touching something else. Myra holds her hands out in the same way but so they won't touch anything else and get that dirty. I thought that was a really great observation but so far I haven't found anybody else who shares my enthusiasm for the phenomena.

Myra moves heavy furniture at home and recently helped load huge musical instruments into a truck during a rainstorm when we needed to move it prior to a school band concert. She can use jumper cables to start stalled cars. Although I lovingly call her "Super Myra," I continue to open doors for her and treat her as the real lady that she is.

Vulnerability—We know that many diseases are caused by viruses which are passed from one person to another who is in close contact. One way to be sure to never catch these diseases is to never allow other people to get close to you. In the same way, many of the heartaches that we experience in our lives are caused by sharing the trials, tribulations, and traumas of those persons who we love and are close to. We could avoid this by living our lives in such a way that we never allow ourselves to develop close relationships with other people. The more blessed one is with close friends and family, the more vulnerable he becomes to the threat of disease and heartache. Those of us who are blessed with many close friends and a large family will inevitably suffer with them as they have problems during their lifetime and eventually die. That is the price we must pay, but it is better than to never experience joy and love in our lives.

Skunk and Porcupine Type Personalities—I've always wondered if skunks smell bad to themselves and other skunks. My guess is that they have some way of adapting to their own smell so it doesn't offend them. It seems to me that there are many humans who must have made the same adjustment and are totally unaware of how obnoxious and repelling they are to others. Just like skunks, these poor souls pack together and seem to overlook the flaws of each other. The difference between skunks and people is that eventually disagreeable people turn on each other. Maybe we should leave them alone to devour each other much like insects do in the biological farming concept. They might just eradicate each other.

Another thing that I worry about is how a porcupine can have any friends. If you get close to one, you will get stuck, and I've even heard that they can throw their spines if they get upset. I've known a few people who have "porcupine type personalities."

Mowing Lawns—You can tell a great deal about a person's personality by watching him or her mow a lawn. Some people are very creative and every time they mow their lawn they think up a new, and supposedly better, way to do it. Others have a more conservative outlook and are content to either go back and forth or around the perimeter, the same way every time they mow. In the past I thought that the only thing that mattered was whether the grass got cut. Recently I have come to believe that mowing a lawn can be an artistic expression or philosophical statement.

Final Grades—When my life's mortal journey is over, my final chapter is written, the final school bell rings, or worse yet, when I wake up some morning and realize that I am dead, I wonder what kind of grading system God will use. Will it be A,B,C,D,F? Or maybe a simple Pass - Fail or Satisfactory - Unsatisfactory? Will there be such a grade as "Incomplete?" Will we get a second chance to go back and live our life right —like repeating second grade? In our school we are allowing kids to retake tests if they fail them, providing that they can provide some evidence that they have done some type of corrective. Will the Master Teacher work out some way we can retake the test of life before He (or more likely, She) marks down our final score? What will happen to us if we are tardy or show up without a pencil ready to work when "the roll is called up yonder?" I bet we have only one chance. We better make the best of it and be ready for the final judgment. Thank God for Grace. We couldn't make it on our own.

Distance and Speed are Relative—I was down at the service station getting the oil changed and overheard an old man saying that he had to get his car serviced because he and his wife were going on a long trip the next day. They were going to Oskaloosa which is 15 miles away. Distance is relative. Speed is also relative. You experience the sensation of moving when you sit in a stationary vehicle and see the vehicle next to you going backwards. Sometimes when you think you are making progress, it might be because the guy next to you is going backwards.

Runners Like Parking Spots Close To The Track—Running is a great exercise but I can't understand why those who use our track think they have to drive on the grass and park right up next to the track instead of in the hard surfaced parking lot. With all of the rains lately the ground has gotten soft and spongy and they cause huge tire tracks. If exercise is what they want, they could get a little more of a good thing by running back and forth from the parking lot to the track. I've also noticed that the walkers and health advocates take up the best parking spaces at the mall and at the YMCA.

Life Is Like—Forest Gump quoted his mother as saying, "Life is like a box of chocolates, you never know what you will get." I have also found that:

Life is like boxing because in both you could win or get knocked out at any time.

Life is like baseball because in both you can't succeed unless you have the opportunity to play. In both baseball and life you could get picked off base at any time and three strikes and you should be out. When a baseball game goes into extra innings in the seventh game of the World Series the manager might say, "At this stage in the game there is no reason to save anything back; you might as well use all that you have." That same philosophy makes sense when a person reaches old age.

Life is like football because in both no one person can get the job done by himself and planning and teamwork are essential.

Life is like running a race because in both you need to get off to a good start and kick it in near the finish line.

Life is like taking a journey because in both you need a well maintained vehicle (physical body) to ride in. You also need to have a plan and know where you want to go (have direction).

What Is Happiness?—Our next door neighbor keeps his dog in a pen. The dog paces back and forth in the small pen and looks lonesome and unhappy to me. Sometimes he howls and on those occasions, I feel like I want to go out and let him out of his jail-like existence. I know that keeping dogs in pens is accepted practice and that dogs can't be allowed to just roam around the neighborhood damaging other people's property, but it still causes me to do some deep thinking. If we had to define dog happiness, what would it be? What about cows? They can't enjoy standing on top of a hill in the winter, with snow flying all around them, and nearly freezing to death! Or is there such a concept as enjoy for dogs and cows? How about moles? Do they enjoy anything and what would "mole happiness" be, living under the ground as they do? Are moles exempt from the concept of empathy? But more importantly what is human happiness? What do we really want out of life? I suppose the answer would be different for each individual. There must be some common denominators that include physical comfort, sex, freedom, and companionship. I know I need to be around other people. Maybe us common guys have some ideas on the subject that need to be brought out. Maybe we shouldn't leave stuff like this to the intellectual elite. They would naturally have a different slant on life than we do. Enough of that. It is getting too deep.

Searching For The Elusive IT—Some people believe that you can really have IT all if you work hard enough, take advantage of every opportunity, and adhere to mindless dedication to procedure. If getting IT is the goal, one must define what IT is. If we can't define IT, how will we know if it is true when someone says, "He has IT made," "That's IT," "What is IT," "You're IT," or "If you work hard, you can do IT." The assumption has already been made that IT is desirable before knowing what IT is. We must ask ourselves what price we should be willing to pay to achieve IT. Before working hard to attain IT, one might ask those who have attained IT: Is IT worth IT, and what is the cost of maintaining IT? In the final analysis one must decide whether to go for IT. Are you better off with IT or without IT? Once you have IT can you ever get back to the way IT was before? Perhaps IT is like the forbidden fruit in the garden of Eden—once you try IT, you've had IT!

Most parents, especially parents of "gifted" students, are convinced that there really is an IT and will not rest until their child has IT. This researcher has determined that IT is an old wives' tale. I searched and couldn't find any wives with tails.

Character Test—When we attempt to evaluate how well our students are progressing toward reaching the outcomes that we have determined that they should reach, we give them a test. Of course, we can't include everything on the test so we pick sample items that we feel reflect our overall objectives. What if the same thing is true when we are all held accountable at the end of our life's journey? What sample questions will be on our "final exam" in the course called Character? We all know that we are expected to obey the Ten Commandments but what else? How about the following?

(1)   You are driving your car and observe a dead animal lying in the middle of the road. You—

    A. Stop on the shoulder of the road, get out the broom that you carry in your trunk, and sweep the carcass off the road.

    B. Proceed on to your destination. When you get there, you call the street department to report the problem.

    C. Drive around the obstacle and forget it.

    D. Try to hit the animal with the car tires so it will spread over more of the road.

(2)   You go to the grocery store. After you park your car in the parking lot you—

A. Collect as many grocery carts as possible together and push them back to the store. Later you push the cart that you used back to the store.

B. Report to the store manager that grocery carts are cluttering up the parking lot.

C. Leave the situation exactly as you found it. Take the cart you used back to the store but no others. You didn't take them out there so why should you take them back?

D. Push your groceries to your car and leave the cart in the parking lot.

(3)   You use the public restroom. After using the facilities you—

A. Flush the one you soiled and as many others as need it.

B. Flush the one you soiled and report any needed attention to the authorities.

C. Flush what you soil and no more.

D. Soil but don't flush

(4)   You notice that little bits of broken glass are covering part of the parking lot. You-

A. Get the broom and dust pan out of your trunk and clean up the glass.(Yes, the same broom that you used to push the dead animal off the road—by now it has a definite odor).

B. Call the person in charge of the area to report the broken glass.

C. Do nothing.

D. Get mad because you realize that your glass coffee cup has broken and then drive off.

Grading scale:

If you answered A for all questions you receive an "A." You are the Answer or solution to problems.

If you answered B for all questions you receive a "B." You are a Bureaucrat, you refer problems to others for solutions. You make sure that there will always be jobs available for others.

If you answered C for all questions you receive a "NI." You make No Impact. The National Park Service would love you. Your death will neither make the world better nor worse. You are currently part of the walking dead.

If you answered D for all questions you receive a "P." You are a part of the problem, or a "NN" because you are a "net negative" person.

Worst Fears—My truck would hardly run. I had visions of a blown head gasket, a faulty transmission, and a series of other serious motor problems. It was only a matter of time before I would have to take it to a mechanic to get the bad news but I put off the inevitable as long as I could. I finally decided that the time had come when the sad truth must be faced. I was prepared to pay a huge bill or worse yet, admit that my old friend was past being useful and ready for the salvage yard. The mechanic discovered that a spark plug wire had come loose. He hooked the wire back up and the truck ran fine. I was relieved that the mechanic found something wrong because it would have been terrible if he had told me that my truck just ran that way and I would have to accept it. I had no idea that the problem might be so minor and easily fixed. That is the way with most of our problems. It is too bad that we don't take care of them sooner instead of worrying so much.

Golf Courses—I never feel comfortable around country clubs or any other type of golf course. When I was a kid, I worked several summers as a caddy at the most exclusive country club in Topeka. To this day, when I am around a golf course, I identify more with the employees than with the members. I expect someone to tap me on the shoulder and say, "Boy, carry my clubs." We had an administrator's party at the country club. It was made clear that I was expected to wear a suit and tie. That was about the only thing that was clear to me about the arrangements. I told Myra that, because we were in such a fancy place and the food and drink prices would be high, to order the lowest priced thing on the menu and only to drink water. We both acted like we really were not hungry and ordered sandwiches for $3.50. When the social affair was over, the lady in charge announced that because no one had kept track of what each of us had eaten, we would just divide the bill up evenly. Our share was $22.00 each or a total of $44.00. It reminded me of the time, many years ago, when I went to my first out of town administrators meeting. I stayed in a cheap old flea trap of a hotel for $5.00. I thought that we would get paid a set amount for lodging and I would come out ahead. I discovered later that the guy that stayed in a $25.00 room got reimbursed $25.00 and I got my $5.00 back.

The Bug Zapper–During all of this cold weather I sit and dream of the warm, sunny summertime. Sometimes during the summer I would like to come in the house and watch TV but I know that the long winter is coming so I feel almost obligated to sit outside when I can. I think how great it was last summer to sit in the shade in my lawn chair drinking lemonade. I also dream of those wonderful summer nights when I engaged in my favorite pastime of watching the bug zapper. It gets to be a real serious concern when I notice that several of the neighbors are getting zappers and I worry about running out of bugs. All of the grandkids and I let out a big "ooh" and "wow" when a super big bug sizzles. I thought about hanging our new bug zapper just outside of our dining room window, next to the bird feeders, so I could sit inside and watch it during bad weather, but I was reluctantly convinced that it would scare the birds away and that bugs don't come in the winter. I even wrote the following poem while contemplating and philosophizing one particularly inspiring night.

Bug Zapper

A mosquito at night, flies straight to the light,
And the "bug zapper" zaps it in the midst of its flight.
Our children are drawn by the bright light of drugs,
Let us hope that people are smarter than bugs.

Technology—I had a nice visit with Elsie Wilson at the church picnic last night. Elsie retired in the late 1950s after teaching elementary school for over thirty years, mostly in one-room school houses. She told me that one year the biggest issue in the community concerned whether or not to have a telephone installed at the school. Some patrons felt strongly that the school should stick to the basics of education and they could not see how having a telephone had anything to do with that mission. Furthermore, it was expensive and taxes could not be raised any more or the whole nation would fall apart at the seams. How could the taxpayers be assured that a telephone would be used properly? What controls would be put in place? The wild liberals prevailed and a telephone was installed. The next year the major issue was a proposal to purchase a movie projector. Some other schools in the county had made the leap and several of the most highly paid teachers were considered experts in the use of audio-visual aids. They knew how to run a 16 mm projector and were willing to provide training. The big decision to purchase a movie projector was made only after Elsie promised to take training on how to use it at her own expense and to show "movies" at least twice a week. These "movies" were rented free of charge from the University of Kansas and were mainly about Navajo Indians, industrialization, and modern farming techniques. Each year Elsie designated an older male student, usually one who didn't experience much success in English and math but was dependable and "good with his hands," as the class audio-visual expert. She kept in contact with many of these guys for years and she claims that, as a group, they are very successful adults.

I guess times haven't changed all that much. We're still arguing about technology. The nature of the technology is different but resistance to using it remains. Paying for it is still an issue and we continue to use it more as a gimmick, separate from the rest of the curriculum, than as a tool to help us do our job better.

The Need to Move Toward Independence —"No man is an island." We are all, at the same time, dependent, interdependent, and independent in our relationships with others.

When a child is born, it can exist only for a few hours without the care of others. It is totally dependent. Mature, contributing members of any society exist in a state of inter-dependence. Each individual contributes the fruits of his unique abilities and capabilities and, in return, depends on others to meet his needs in other areas.

Moving from the childhood stage of life to adulthood should be characterized by becoming dependent in less ways and moving to more interdependence and independence. Our goal should be to contribute more to our families, communities, and world than we consume from them.

There need not be the same quantity of take as give in a group. It is not like filling a cup with water and the cup must always have water poured out to accept any water that is added. It is not like an athletic event where for every winner there must be a loser. In any group the container for good will and contributing is infinite, endlessly elastic, and has no full mark.

We all need help from other people but when this help results in contributing to that person becoming more dependent on us and less able to meet his own needs, we are hurting rather than helping the very person that we care so much for. Need is the great motivator. When we feel a need for something, and are allowed by others to do whatever is necessary to meet our need, we grow toward being less dependent on others. When others intervene in our behalf, we learn to be more dependent.

Most parents love their children so much that they have a very difficult time observing their children wrestling with the day-to-day pressures of life. Sometimes parents step in and do things to make their child's life at that moment less stressful and as a result make their child more dependent and more of a "taker" than "giver." Many well meaning social programs result in those targeted for help becoming more dependent. These well intentioned programs have long-range negative effects. When we help others, we must always analyze whether we are really helping or hurting them. Love and care can cause us to do just the opposite of what we intend to do.

People are different from audio cassette records. A full audio cassette tape can easily be transferred to a blank tape. This can be done quickly by using two tape decks and fast dubbing. Some adults would like to transfer their own thoughts, feelings, morals, attitudes, and experiences to a child in this manner. They see themselves as the full tape and the child as a blank tape. This just does not work. Each individual person has a mind of his own. This concept is what the story of Adam and Eve in the Garden of Eden is all about.

School Security—We have all witnessed the look of complete and absolute security, safety, satisfaction and bliss on the face of a young child who is being held in the loving arms of his or her mom or dad. If we are lucky we can remember experiencing that same warm glow and sense of peace ourselves. The troubles of the world seemed remote and far away. Long after we become chronologically and officially adults, the child in all of us continues to yearn to be comforted in such a loving manner. Oh, to once more be held in the strong arms of our dad, our invincible hero, who we know will protect us from all evil forces! How wonderful it would be, no matter how old we might be, to once more be gently and softly hugged by our doting mom, carried up the stairs, kissed, and tucked into bed. Although both of my parents have passed on to heaven many years ago, sometimes when things go wrong it helps me to look at an old picture of them and imagine that they are once more holding me. We never outgrow the need to be accepted, just as we are, and feel completely and unconditionally loved. When we experience the Grace of God and the closeness of Christ during church worship services, we gain a clearer understanding of the essence of the meaning behind the words of the old hymn, "Children of the Heavenly Father, Safely in his Bosom Gather." If only there could be some way that we could create that same atmosphere in our classrooms, and in the whole school environment. That would be real "School Security."

Getting Plugged In—Educators must be "plugged in" to others to maintain the power necessary to exist in a tough career. My bug zapper didn't come on one evening and I searched my mind for what might be the problem. I had recently replaced one of the bulbs so that shouldn't be the problem. Maybe the power bar that it was plugged into had blown or, worse yet, maybe something was wrong with the outlet in the garage. Then I remembered that I had unplugged the power bar that the bug zapper was plugged into a few nights earlier because of a rain storm. Upon further examination I discovered that when I plugged the power bar back in I had plugged it into itself instead of into the wall socket. Both power bars and people need to be plugged into something besides themselves if they are to have the power to function.

School Administration and Lightning Rods—The principal of a school, or head of any organization, must understand that because of the very nature of the leadership role that he/she plays, the administrator will function for the organization very much in the same way that a lightning rod functions for a building.

The static electricity that forms when positive and negative charges rub against each other during a rain storm does not fall harmlessly to the earth spread equally over the entire area, but rather it gathers together and travels to the earth in the form of a single lightning bolt directed at one specific point. This bolt of lightning, instead of randomly hitting a home and causing severe damage, can be received by a lightning rod and, in a controlled manner, be directed to the ground. The lightning rod must be firmly grounded if it is to do what it is made to do. All of the electrical outlets in a building must also be well grounded or a fire could result that could cause much damage. When there is no turbulence light rain or snow falls gently and evenly to the earth and there is no need for a lightning rod.

In the same manner, the leader of any group must expect to function as a lightning rod for the group or institution that he or she leads. Positive and negative charges that naturally and surely form are always present around any group. Under normal conditions, when everything is calm, these charges fall equally distributed over the entire group. When there is turbulence, and these positive and negative forces start to rub each other wrong, a bolt of input is funneled to the one person who, as an individual, personifies the whole institution. If that person is well grounded the charges will be handled properly and will dissipate. If not, damage will surely occur. The leader of the group, like the lightning rod, must be made of strong and durable material or burn-out will occur and it/he will need to be replaced on a regular basis. Just as all of the electrical outlets in a building must be well grounded, all of the staff members of a school must also be well grounded or they cannot serve adequately as sources of power (learning).

A good leader is a person who takes a little more than his share of the blame and a little less than his share of the credit. The "lightning rod" concept is that the leader will inevitably receive more of both than is really deserved.

Know His Voice—The staff of a school will follow the principal only if they "know his voice," that is, if they have experienced his or her leadership and the principal has gained or earned respect and credibility. The following quote from the Bible expresses it well: "Sheep will follow the Shepherd for they know his voice." John 10, verse 4. The following old cowboy quote also makes the same point: "If you get to thinkin' you're a person of some influence, try orderin' someone else's dog around."

Other quotes in the Bible ring a bell also, but not in such a positive way. Like sometimes, after a particularly tough day at school, I think Psalm 31 beginning with verse 9 could have been written about a school principal. It could be called the "School Administrator's Psalm." It reads: "Be gracious to me, Oh Lord, for I am in distress; my eye is wasted from grief, my soul and my body also. For my life is spent with sorrow, and my years with sighing; my strength fails because of my misery, and my bones waste away. I am the scorn of all my adversaries, a horror to my neighbors, an object of dread to my acquaintances; those who see me in the street flee from me. I have passed out of mind like one who is dead; I have become like a broken vessel. Yea, I hear the whispering of many—terror on every side! as they scheme together against me, as they plot to take my life." Maybe this Psalm overstates the case a little, but most of us can identify with at least certain parts of it.

Administrators—To Serve or to be served? Is the principal the King or Queen of the school? Is he or she to be served by others? Should all others be required to ask permission to exist within his or her kingdom which is the school? Should he or she be assigned the best parking place, have someone serve refreshments and make coffee, and expect others of lower rank to clean up after him/her? Should all others be expected to adjust their calendars so that they can see the principal at his/her convenience? Is the social order in a school from the top down—administrator, staff, student? Does the principal have rank and unquestioned authority? Can he/she make decisions without consulting anyone else because he/she holds the power and what others think doesn't matter? Should everyone be expected to obey the principal's commands without question? Or on the other hand—

Should the principal be expected, even more than other school employees, to function as a public servant? Are students the real reason that schools exist and therefore, like customers in private businesss, the ones in the school to be served?

It has been written that power corrupts and absolute power corrupts absolutely. Principals must be constantly reminded that they are not Rulers—they are servants. The real bosses in a school are the taxpayers. The purpose of schools is to serve students. Therefore, the most important persons in any school are the students. Those public servants who work directly with students are second in importance. The principal must be a public servant in the superlative sense. He is among those on the staff whose job is to make sure that teachers are able to do the job of teaching by making sure that an environment conducive for learning exists. He is the teacher's teacher. The principal is usually the highest paid person on the staff, therefore more is expected of him than of anyone else on the staff. The public expects to get what they pay for. If it needs to be done, the principal should either do it himself or see that it gets done. Principals would be expected to know, even more than other school employees, that parents and visitors must have the best parking spots reserved for them. The next best parking spots should be reserved for staff members who work directly with students. What is left should be used by the principal, because he is the "most servant of all."

A college football coach was quoted in Sports Illustrated magazine as saying, "You just can't feel totally a part of an event unless you participate in planning it, carrying it out, and cleaning up after it." A true leader must be involved in all three of these phases. Using a mop or broom should not be beneath the dignity of the school principal.

Some principals could be categorized as "Old Testament type administrators." They exist to follow the Law (policy). Others believe in following the Law (policy) but put an even higher priority on serving people and the spirit of doing what is right. They are "New Testament type administrators." It is not what a man does that determines whether his work is sacred or secular; it is why he does it. The two Bible verses quoted below help to explain this concept:

> "Jesus called them to him and said, 'You know that the rulers of the Gentiles lord it over them, and their great men exercise authority over them. It shall not be so among you: but whoever would be great among you must be your servant, and whoever would be first among you must be your slave: even as the Son of Man came not to be served but to serve, and to give his life as a ransom for many.'" Matthew 20:25-28 RSV

"Do not use your freedom as an opportunity for self-indulgence, but through love become slaves to one another." I Peter 2:16-17 NRSV

"For the whole law is summed up in a single commandment, 'You shall love your neighbor as yourself.'" Matthew 19:19 RSV

Administrators and Mouthwashes—I've noticed that some of my administrator friends continue to think that school administrators are like mouthwashes. They both must leave a bad taste in the mouth if they are doing a good job. For years I used a particular mouthwash that tasted bad because I had been convinced that those that left a nice minty taste in my mouth couldn't possibly both kill germs and taste good as if carrying out one of these functions was mutually exclusive of the other. What a great relief it was to discover that administrators, like mouthwashes, can both do a good job and leave a good taste in a person's mouth. It's too bad that some administrators spend a lifetime thinking that they must play the role of martyr and that being disliked just goes with standing up for "what is right" and that some day a grateful community will honor them for being so nasty.

The Vice-Principal's Role—Last night we held our annual new student and parent orientation. All of the hard work that I do during the summer making an individual schedule for each student, assigning locks and lockers, and printing up a new student handbook finally comes together on this one glorious night. We could feel the excitement and tension in the

air. The secretaries, my vice-principal, and I were putting the finishing
touches on the computer print-outs. I looked out of the window and could
see the crowd coming to take their places in the bleachers in the gym to
hear my well prepared welcoming speech. I experienced the familiar rush
of excitement and feeling of anxious anticipation that I felt years ago just
before playing in a basketball game or running in a track meet. In athletic
competition it was comforting to know that I had the backing of my
teammates. Now I am thankful that I can count on my vice-principal to
back me up if I need it.

A good vice-principal plays many roles. He is both an idea man,
who is expected to come up with new ideas himself, and an honest and
frank idea filter for the principal's ideas. It is desirable to get as many
impurities as possible out of ideas before they pass through other less
understanding idea filters out there in the public. Just as in the movies
they have stand-ins for actors when the script calls for a dangerous act, the
vice principal sometimes is called to stand-in as a stunt man for the
principal when the going gets tough. A vice-principal is the principal's
private counselor and right arm. He or she gets things done. Just as a
boxer needs a good cut man in his corner to repair damage done to his face
between rounds during a fight, a principal occasionally needs a good vice-
principal to restore damage done to his reputation during an especially
difficult parent conference. In the old days when the covered wagons
traveled across the prairie, one person drove the team and another person
was designated to ride shotgun. His role was to cover the driver when the
going got tough. In the same way, a vice-principal has to ride shotgun for
the principal. He is also counted on to be the principal's booger man to let
him know when he has a booger on his collar or egg on his face and
doesn't realize it or, in other words, needs to clean up his act. He fulfills
the same function for the principal that a spotter,does for a gymnast, he
stands by to help as needed while the principal does his act. He must be a
teacher's teacher. Good vice-principals dutifully carry out all of these roles
and can expect the same from any principal worth his salt.

The Superintendent's Balancing Act—The superintendent of
schools is constantly walking a tightrope to make sure that he adequately
fills the role of both Chief Executive Officer of the Board of Education and
leader of district personnel. If he leans too far one way or the other, he will
fall on his face. He can't neglect either one for long and survive.

Unlike other employees of a school district, the superintendent
works directly for the Board of Education (BOE). The BOE determines his
salary and controls his job security. He works at their pleasure. Therefore,
he must carry out their wishes or suffer the consequences. The BOE pays

the piper so they get to pick the tune.

On the other hand, the Superintendent is the primary leader of the staff. He is the coach of the team, general of the troops, teacher's teacher, and instructional leader. He can't lead unless someone follows. The boss can delegate responsibilities, but not relationships. To lead the group he must first be a part of it. He must be accepted and respected by the troops and he must take care of them.

It is easy to find a great Superintendent. Just find someone with the wisdom of Solomon, the heart of Sister Theresa, and the emotional toughness of a Teflon coated frying pan. Anyone who works for the public and thinks he answers to no one will soon find out that he answers to everyone.

Wrathing—The Pick Of The Litter Method—During the first few years that a person serves as a principal, each and every crisis experience is a new and emotion evoking adventure. Adrenalin flows abundantly, eyes gleam, passion is aroused, lips tremble, and the stomach churns. The young administrator jumps directly into action and does something with sincere enthusiasm and zeal. Students receive the needed bawling out. Teachers feel that the administrator truly understands the seriousness of the problem and identifies with them. Parents are alerted that they cannot intimidate the school personnel.

The young administrator wants to convey the message that "I run a tight ship and don't allow any foolishness." His actions are automatic, springing up from the shock of the act committed. He operates on an emotional gut-feeling level and off the seat of his pants. Actions follow emotional responses so rapidly that there is no time to consider alternatives on the conscious level. He does not consciously and deliberately decide that a mad act is needed. He simply gets mad. Sometimes his actions get him into trouble and he is constantly being threatened with law suits. He spends much time after he acts, justifying what he did because his actions were not planned and consciously thought out.

After a few years of working as a building administrator, a special kind of adaptation takes place. He is able to get off the emotional roller coaster. He finds that, like a popular prostitute or a professional basketball player, he has a difficult time arousing passion and strong emotion on demand. He has experienced almost every kind of crisis repeatedly. An administrator whose job description includes handling student discipline in a large secondary school could possibly chastise a different student every ten minutes. Things get routine, similar to a barber cutting hair and then calling for the next customer.

Unfortunately, the public seems to feel that one of the major roles

that a school principal should play in the community is to "wreak
vengeance on the wicked." Students, teachers, and parents need, expect,
and on occasion demand that administrators display righteous indignation
and convey with fire in their eyes how things will be! There is no question
but that wrath is called for. Most people would really rather be the
righteous wrath-er than the wrath-ee, but redundant reeking of wrath can
become nerve wrecking. In order to be effective, the show must go on. A
convincing "mad act," with an emphasis on sternness, must be prepared
and performed. Over the years, he develops his own personal "lecture
series" which covers every possible infraction that comes his way.

The experienced administrator is not programmed to respond
automatically with emotion. He operates on a conscious mental level. He
quickly analyzes what reaction would be appropriate and acts accordingly.
Instead of stimulus-action; the pattern now becomes stimulus-conscious
deliberation-action. Because the process now involves the conscious level
of thought, actions are usually quite effective and appropriate. A planned,
prepared, and rehearsed act is used rather than an extemporaneous reaction.

The conscious level of thought acts as a filter. Only actions that
are appropriate and defensible get through this filter. When an
administrator calmly and deliberately chooses his behavior, he will usually
select the pick of the litter action, the best or, at worst, the least bad method
of resolving the problem. This is to practice Safe Administration (to
borrow from sex education) and Defensive Education (to borrow from
driver's education). When we interview for a new vice-principal, we
should ask him or her to give us a "wrathing demonstration."

Keep The Other Guy Wrong—I spent the entire morning
preaching to kids that when someone does something bad or wrong, you
have them right where you want them. They are wrong and you are right.
Because of this, everyone will agree with you when you say that they
should be punished. It is only right and just that they receive some
negative consequences. They should receive no pity from anyone and they
deserve whatever happens to them. Any reasonable person would side with
you against them.

However, if you do the same thing, or worse, in retaliation, you
are just as guilty as they are, and you lose your advantage. School
principals want to back their staff members but are sometimes thwarted by
the fact that what the staff member did or said to a student is just as
indefensible as the original act of the student. When two students have a
conflict, they like to turn the issue into a "who started it" mode. What they
need to understand is that all acts will need to be considered, not just the
first act. Wrong reactions are just as bad as wrong actions. The real trick is

to keep the other guy wrong and consciously choose not to allow yourself to do anything that you may need to say you are sorry for at a later date.

For example, the night custodian came to me and told me that a student who was in the building late last night swore at him when he was told that he must leave the building. I asked the janitor what he did when that happened. He said, "I cussed him out, grabbed him, slapped him a few times, and threw him out of the door." I suggested that it might be difficult to defend punishing the student for swearing because the janitor had done the same and worse. The janitor walked off muttering something about the poor quality of kids that we have in school these days.

The janitor had the kid right where he wanted him when the kid had done something wrong and the janitor had not. He could have told me about the incident the next day and would have received my complete support. The kid could then have been punished and justice would have prevailed. Our whole case was blown when the janitor reacted in the same way that the kid had acted. The old saying is true: two wrongs don't make a right.

Idea Filters—We all depend daily on filters to purify the air that we breathe, the water that we drink, and the oil that lubricates the motor of the cars we drive. In the same way, our plans and ideas should be subject to being filtered though a series of "idea filters." Often an idea or procedure that at first glance looks to be free of impurities, upon closer scrutiny, contains some small imperfections that should be removed, or at least considered, before implementation. Educators should use other people as idea filters as often as possible. After an idea has passed through as many filters as possible, most of its faults will have been removed and, if anything still exists, and you still believe that it will work, try it.

Skinning the Softball Diamonds—I started my school administration career back in the early 1960s. At that time the PTA came to me and suggested that we skin the softball diamonds on the south playground. It made sense to me. Real ball diamonds have dirt infields not grass. It would be a definite step toward progress. At the March parent group meeting we asked for volunteers and started raising enough money to pay for some large equipment to come in and tear away the grass. Several large dump trucks full of the recommended clay type dirt were brought in. Finally, we leveled it with rakes and used some lawn tractors to drag a large metal grate that we had made over it. Then we stood back and admired our work. Soon it was summer and the south wind started to blow and the heavy rains fell. The name "Kansas" means "land of the south winds." Dust covered the school inside and out and the same was true for every house within a block of the school. It wasn't long before the dirt that we had hauled in to put on the softball diamonds had either been blown away by the hot wind or washed away by the heavy rains. Much of our softball season was called off because of muddy grounds and, worse yet, a growing number of people had let their opinion be known that they didn't appreciate the dust in their homes. Even the teachers were upset because they either had to suffer and not open up the windows when it got hot in the classrooms or get the room covered with dust. I regretted that I had arranged for the speaker on assertiveness training at the May PTA meeting. Something had to be done. At the September PTA meeting we again asked for volunteers and we again raised money to have dirt hauled in. Only this time it was top soil. We leveled the dirt out with rakes and planted grass. We spent the next few weeks watering the grass and soon had a grass covered infield. It was almost but not quite as good as the one we had before we skinned it.

Nine years passed. I moved over to the middle school. At an administrators meeting the new elementary principal told how proud he was that he and the PTA had just completed skinning the softball diamonds on the south playground. I smiled and kept my thoughts to myself. If they had passed this idea through the administrative meeting filter, I could have told them what to expect. They probably would have proceeded as planned anyway because nobody likes to have cold water thrown on their plans, especially by someone from the past, but at least they would have had the opportunity to take a fresh look at the idea with south wind and rain as factors.

I told this true story to my son who is a math teacher. He said that in higher math circles the terms for reoccurring phenomena like this are sine waves and periodic functions.

Another similar thing happened in Chicago back in the 1970s. A young and innovative principal received merit pay for changing the old six period day to a system were no bells ring and there are no set periods. Nine years later another young and innovative principal took over and received merit pay for saving the same school from a chaotic situation by initiating a conservative system which featured strict discipline and a six period day. What goes around, comes around!

Sloping Soap Dish Solutions—The housekeeping department of a major hotel chain convinced the maintenance department to install soap dishes in the hotel showers at a sloping angle so that water would not stand in them. The housekeeping department didn't want to spend their time wiping out soap dishes. The idea was presented to the national management of the hotel chain and approved. Sloping soap dishes were installed in thousands of shower stalls all over the nation.

While the sloping soap dish did accomplish the desired purpose of promoting dryer soap dishes, it also soon became obvious that it had one major flaw—wet bars of soap slid right off of them. They didn't hold soap! Hotel guests soon complained loudly about the inconvenience of constantly having to bend over in the shower to pick up slippery bars of soap. Unfortunately, before changes could be made some major law suits were filed against the hotel. Guests had fallen and broken bones while bending over to pick up soap. Several major lessons can be learned from this experience:

(1) Holding soap is the one and only purpose of soap dishes. No one checked to see if the sloping soap dishes could carry out the function of holding soap. When making changes make sure that you promote rather than detract from your stated mission. Too often changes in schools do not take into consideration how they affect the purpose of the school which is to promote student learning. "How will it affect students?" must be asked every time some change is made in a school. Just as "How will it effect bars of soap and hotel guests?" should have been asked by the hotel management in the example given here.

(2) Try sloping one real soap dish to see how it works before you change all of them. In the school setting changes should be piloted by one real teacher and with only a limited number of students. If changes create the desired effect with a few, expand them to affect others.

Sounds and Sights in a Middle School—-Watch carefully and you can see the bright light bulb flash in the head of a student as he suddenly grasps an understanding of some concept or idea. If you watch closely you can actually see the eighth grade boys grow, usually one part at a time. If you listen carefully, you can hear the seventh grade girls' busts busting and the ninth grade boys' hormones moaning. Females come into middle school as caterpillars and leave as butterflies. In elementary school the girls fought to play with the same toy; now in middle school they fight to play with the same boy. You can observe both complete ecstasy and deep depression on the same day in the same kid. Happy voices, laughs, and giggles in the lunchroom, loud screaming in the gymnasium, muffled whispering and sobs in the girls' rest room (the unofficial or peer counselor's office) combine to create the daily sights and sounds of the middle school. Individual differences are the name of the game. Tapping on the desk, bouncing the leg until the whole room shakes, "We were just playing around," "He did it to me first," "Everyone else does it," playing with food, burping just for fun, boys jumping to touch ceilings, girls looking in the mirror, rummaging around in lockers, tapping on the shoulder and then looking the other way, April Fools, not being seen with your mom, pimples, girls at the bus stop waving their arms pretending to be cheerleaders, bumping each other off the end of the bench, acting cool one minute and excited as a kindergartner the next. This is middle school!

They All Want To Play With The Same Toy (Or Boy) — No matter how many toys parents make available to their children, beginning at about age two, they all seem to want to play with the same toy at the same time. You can see the same phenomenon when you watch kids play on the playground. There might be dozens of swings, but they seem to all want the same one. Let a little time pass and the swing that seemed to be so favored earlier will be totally rejected in favor of some other piece of equipment. Many parents have tried to solve this "you must share" problem by purchasing more toys. That doesn't work. The problem is not that there are not enough toys available but rather that kids all want to play with the same toy at the same time. A particular seat in the car can go for miles drawing no interest whatsoever and then, for no apparent reason, it suddenly becomes as valuable as a queen's throne and everyone wants to sit in it. The first kid to use a toy, car seat, or whatever is continually admonished to share. I'm sure that every parent has heard "But I had it first," and replied "That doesn't matter, we all have to share." Why? Why can't the other kids be told to go find something else to play with? Why does everyone on the earth feel that they have a right to stand on the same square foot of ground? If someone else is using something, doesn't it make sense to use something else until they get done with it and then try it if it still seems attractive?

In the middle school setting we find that the tendency of all to want the same thing is just as strong as ever. The "thing" has changed from a toy to something else. It could be clothes, boyfriend or girlfriend, or just a friend. Middle school kids are very possessive of their friends and don't want to share them with anybody. An educator who works with this age of students must be very much aware of these tendencies and not be surprised or upset when conflicts arise. For the most part the best thing to do is deal with the symptoms and with the passage of time, all will return to calm. That is until it all happens all over again and it inevitably will. The only difference is that something or someone else has suddenly become the most prized possession in the world.

The good news is that most people learn to cope with this affliction fairly well. Those who don't just take what they want from other people and are known as criminals. The bad news is that it never seems to go away. Even adults suffer from it. Just let your next door neighbor get something and see if you don't suddenly seem to need it too.

The Staff of a School is Like an Orchestra — The instructional staff of a school is like an orchestra. Each member of an orchestra and each member of the school staff is an expert who specializes at playing a particular role. Individual teachers are experts at teaching in a specialized area of the curriculum. They are well trained and have practiced what they do long and hard. They keep up with the latest trends in their particular fields. They are experts at what they do. Orchestra members are likewise specialists and experts at playing a particular instrument.

An orchestra needs a leader. The orchestra leader may or may not be better at playing any particular instrument than the individual players that he or she directs. The school staff also needs a leader. The principal serves that function. The principal often is not as proficient as the teachers that he directs at doing the specialized things that each of them do.

Music has three basic elements: rhythm, harmony, and melody. A school staff needs to be on the same schedule of getting things done (rhythm), work together (harmony), and be playing the same tune or working toward the same objectives (common melody).

The role that both the orchestra leader and the principal play is to set the beat so that everyone is working together. Both leaders must also determine the volume of the entire group and, when the script calls for it, direct specific individuals for solos or to be featured while the rest of the group plays a background role.

They both demand harmony. Various players will play different notes but the resulting outcome must be in harmony. All participants must be playing in the same key and major or minor mode. The key to an orchestra playing a beautiful tune is that all players do not play the exact same note at the exact same time. Some instruments are larger and emit deep, low, mellow tones. Some are smaller and have a higher and more shrill sound. Woodwinds, brass, string, and percussion instruments each have a unique quality to contribute to the overall beautiful sound that an orchestra makes (its outcome). A school staff needs the same diversity of contribution and a wide range of input from a variety of sources if it is to effectively promote learning (its outcome). If every player in an orchestra plays the same note as the conductor and with the same instrument that the conductor plays, the result will be a monotonous uniformity that lacks beauty and harmony and is not pleasing to the ear. Likewise, if every staff member specializes in the same thing and always takes the same approach to solving problems that the principal takes, the school will lack the vitality needed to adequately meet the needs of a diverse student body.

A building principal needs to set the pace for the school staff just as the orchestra conductor needs to set the pace for the individuals that he directs. He must be able to determine when one staff member or department is playing too loud, too soft, or is out of tune. He must possess the skill to take whatever action is needed to correct problems.

In an orchestra, as in a school, the conductor is only as good as the players make him. From the principal's perspective, the great philosopher Casey Stengel was right when he said, "Ability is the art of getting credit for all of the home runs somebody else hits." The conductor does not personally make any sound whatsoever. Orchestras are judged by the quality of the sound that they make. Both the conductor and the principal must get the job done through the efforts of others. They both depend on each individual member of their team to perform at the highest possible level of excellence. Individual members of the orchestra and of the education team are dependent on the leader to play the role of directing the whole unit so that harmony prevails. No man is an island. We depend on each other.

Just A Drop In The Bucket—We have all heard educators express the feeling that the influence they have on students doesn't matter much because it is "only a drop in the bucket." The reason is that they have students at school for only a very small percentage of their lives. At the secondary level most staff members only have one period of the day to influence any one student. Many teachers are in contact with over a hundred students each day. Administrators feel overwhelmed by the responsibility to influence every student in the school. Educators are by nature sincerely concerned about all of their students, but they wonder how thin they can be spread and feel frustrated that they can't make more of a difference in each student's life.

The bucket is probably mostly filled by parents—both genetically and by early age contact. What children inherit and learn from their parents may be good, or may be bad, but is definitely dominant over other influences.

The good news is that the bucket is filled one drop at a time. Each and every drop is important. The influence of parents is added to that of one teacher which is added to the influence of other teachers. Then is added the influence of YMCA workers, civic club members, church workers, 4-H club leaders, boy and girl scout leaders, recreation workers, coaches, and thousands of other persons who have some kind of relationship with the child over a long period of time. Individual drops in the bucket combine to make a large volume. The entire community in which a person lives has a tremendous influence on each individual that lives in the community.

Each of us would be surprised if we really knew how much influence we have on individual students. They very rarely tell us because they don't quite know how to. They would be embarrassed and are often not capable of articulating the strong feelings of respect and admiration that they feel. Most adults can look back over their lifetimes and pick out individuals who contributed more than just a drop in their buckets. The individuals that we pick out as influencing us never had any idea that they made a difference. Many of them died not knowing what they had accomplished because we never told them.

The greatest compliment a person can receive is to be mentioned as a person who made a difference in the life of an old codger when he engages in rambling reminiscence of his life. Teachers have an opportunity to make a difference that those in other professions do not have. If we act each day in a manner that could result in us being so remembered fifty years from now, we will be successful now.

Just a drop in the bucket. Maybe. But without each drop the bucket would be less full than it is. We get to our destination one inch at a time. We learn one lesson at a time. Our bucket is filled one drop at a time.

Black Sox Solutions "One Size Fits All"— A "Black Sox Solution" is what educators too often make when confronted with the problem of dealing with the needs of a wide variety of students. We decide that conformity is the answer. We determine that we can cope with only one style of teaching, one kind of student, and one curriculum.

The term Black Sox Solution originated one day when a group of male teachers were in the teachers' lounge discussing the problems that result from having a wide variety of stockings. Because these stockings are different colors, styles, textures, brands, and lengths, they must be matched into pairs every time they are washed. Several possible solutions were suggested. Ted said that he pins his sox together in pairs when they are washed so they won't get mixed up with other sox. Bob thought that maybe clothes pins would serve the same function. Ole said that he only buys sox that come with snaps already on them and that he snaps them together in pairs when he puts them in the dirty clothes hamper. Mike suggested that perhaps all sox could be put into a cloth bag when they are washed so they wouldn't get mixed in with other clothes. If you do that it will help some but they will still need to be sorted into pairs. No matter what ideas we came up with, the fact remained that as long as we have diversity and variety in stockings we will always be bothered with the problem of matching. Finally we came to the conclusion that the answer was to purchase a large quantity of the same color, style, texture, brand, and length, of stockings. If all of the stockings were identical, there would be no need to match them into pairs. It was decided that black sox could be worn with just about any combination of clothing. Hence, the Black Sox

Solution. The Black Sox Solution has worked well. The person wearing the sock has the right to decide that he just doesn't want to bother with variety and diversity.

The same concept is a total disaster when applied to teaching. Students just naturally come in different colors, styles, textures, brands, and lengths. Not only that, they come with different needs, interests, backgrounds, and capacities. All students can and will learn but not in the same way. They are undeniably by nature different from each other. Although identical twins may at first appear identical, when you get to know them better, you will discover that they are different in many ways. Far too many educators attempt to apply a Black Sox Solution to the challenge that student diversity creates. The perception that kids can be treated like sox is probably the biggest hurdle that we must overcome if we are to successfully meet the needs of children. Blanket policies that apply to all regardless of the circumstances, a "one size fits all curriculum," and over zealous attempts to be consistent are examples of Black Sox Solutions.

Classroom Instruction Like Aerobics—I watched a television show on aerobics today. The show was designed so that it had three different participants demonstrating the action. One older lady was demonstrating what was called low impact aerobics. She did all of the moves but much slower and with little gusto. Another person demonstrated medium impact aerobics. He moved faster and with more extension of motion but kind of relaxed some. The third person, a young lady in great physical condition, demonstrated what is called high impact aerobics. She moved very rapidly, extended every move to its extreme limit, jumped higher, and in general moved much more than the other two participants. They were in the same room, with the same music, and the same instructor, yet each one was getting a workout that met his or her unique needs and took in consideration where each of them was in relation to that specific activity.

Is it possible that we should try to run our classroom in a way that would take into consideration the reality that we have high, medium, and low impact kids in the room? The same "music" (curriculum) could be provided by the same teacher in the same room but maybe we could allow the kids to participate as high, medium, or low impact depending on their unique characteristics. The way aerobics is taught might just be the best way for most classroom instruction to be taught. Content areas that are highly sequential in nature, like math, some sciences, and foreign languages are more like running a distance where it is best to allow participants to go as fast as they can and not be held back by the slower and less talented. In content areas of that nature the aerobic concept wouldn't work because those involved need to be allowed to spread out and not stay physically together. How should religion be thought of? I think more like aerobics than like the mile run.

The Seven Day Vacation—I was down at the auto salvage yard last Saturday visiting with my son-in-law Curt who runs the place. I ran into Homer Higgins or Junk Yard Homer as he is called. Homer's regular job is to head up the computer department for a large company. He loves to spend his time off at the salvage yard just hanging around. Curt sees the salvage yard as work but Homer sees the same thing as loads of fun and the place to spend as much time as possible. Homer knows the business as well as any of the employees and he answers the phone and otherwise chips in and helps as is needed.

Homer and I started the usual Kansas small talk about the weather, families, and sports. Then I asked him whether he had gone on a vacation yet this year. He told me that he and his wife were planning to go on a vacation the week of November 10th. I asked him where they planned to go this year. He said they were going on a "seven day vacation." They will just drive wherever they want to for three and a half days and then turn around and come home the next three and a half days. He said they hadn't even talked about where they would go as they just had the desire to get away from all of the "locked in structure, time restraints, strict schedules, decision making, and the lack of freedom and flexibility" that he experiences all year at his job. His wife is a doctor and also feels the need to do whatever she wants for a week and just really enjoy life.

My first reaction to this plan was very positive. Just think of the fun and freedom. Then I visualized my wife and I sitting in the driveway early in the morning on the first day of our vacation. We would immediately be forced to make a major decision—which direction to start driving. If we went east, we wouldn't get to see the Rocky Mountains. If we went west, we wouldn't get to go to the Nashville Now show. Our desire had been to get away from decision making for a week and here we are forced to make the one decision that will determine what the rest of our vacation will be like before we even leave our driveway. And, even worse, now we don't even have the time to make the decision after considering alternatives. The decision would have to be made now.

After we drive for a while we would eventually need to stop for a night at a motel. What if all the motels are full? I remembered that time a few years ago when our whole family was forced to sleep in the car out in Arizona because every motel that we came to had the dreaded "No Vacancy" sign up. We woke up tired and grumpy with no shower available. What if we happened to end up in a place where the only entertainment available is a rodeo and I wanted to go to a baseball game and my wife likes music shows. What if after we drove 100 miles west, we decided that we really wanted to go east? What if we didn't end up where we had always deep down wanted to go?

I decided that the plan (or lack of a plan) was not for me. Consciously reflecting on what both my wife and I enjoyed and wanted to accomplish on our vacation and then cooperatively setting some goals would be a better idea. Much of the enjoyment in any activity is in planning it. Making decisions before it is necessary to act makes decision making easier rather than taking away my freedom. Instead of being seen in a negative way, the term "time restraints" can become an agreed upon itinerary. A schedule is a useful tool to use in order to be sure that we are able to get to all of the places we want to get to. Making motel reservations in advance simply reassures us that we will have a place to sleep comfortably every night.

An analogy can be made between the "seven day vacation" story and our experience in providing educational opportunities for students. Sometimes we verbalize the desire to have academic freedom, flexibility, and get away from the practice of setting goals that constrain us. We shy away from making decisions prior to the teaching/learning act. We say that we wish to make those decisions only when they need to be made. If we consider all of the problems that the unplanned approach can get us into, we will agree that setting goals and deciding on desired outcomes before we start to teach is the best approach. Setting goals in a calm, deliberate, considered, reflective, cooperative manner can be of great service to us and make our job much easier and effective. We can't expect to get to a certain place unless we decide where to start out. If we know in advance where we want to get to (our outcome) we can decide how to best get there. Schedules, structure, daily plans, desired outcomes, and an itinerary are all tools that help to get us where we want to go. We should see them in a positive way as things that serve us, not in a negative way as things that restrict or constrain us.

The great sports writer Grantland Rice wrote, "When the One Great Scorer comes to write against your name, He marks, not that you won or lost, but how you played the game." It helps us to play the game better if we have a plan.

The GUMBALL MACHINE COMPLEX—Myra and I were driving our granddaughter, Heather Lewis age 4, to Sunday School. Heather and three other grandchildren were settled in the car when I asked Heather, "How are you today, Heather?" Heather replied angrily, "Not Beary Good! Erin got three things out of the gumball machine and I only got two." According to Heather's mother the Lewis family had visited friends in Wichita a week earlier and the gumball incident had occurred.

Heather had not mentioned it since but had been visibly upset at times. The incident was a minor one in the eyes of everyone but Heather. She had been quietly mad for a week.

In every classroom there are students who are experiencing the Gumball Machine Complex. They feel that they have been gypped in some way. They only got a little bit of something and they see others who got more. Maybe other girls are cheerleaders and they are not. Possibly they feel that they got the short end of the stick because their families are not economically well off. They may feel that they are physically weaker or less attractive than others. Sometimes the problem could be something that to others seems very minor but is very important to the person who feels gypped. The condition can be a very mild case causing only a bad attitude for a short period of time or so serious that it leads to suicide.

We should always be alert to the possibility that others with whom we have contact may be experiencing the Gumball Machine Complex and help them deal with it.

Some People Really Do Have a Fork In Their Chair—I've noticed that when you tether a dog, it will spend most of its time at the outer limits of the rope, pulling, barking, and wanting to go further. It is the same with people. No matter how liberal the limits are that are placed on them, they are unhappy and spend much of their time and energy complaining and begging to have the limits broadened. Nobody likes people who continually complain, whine, and gripe. It seems like much of what I do in my job involves listening to people tell me what is wrong. Sometimes it seems that the best thing that happens to me is that I get a wrong number phone call. It gets tiresome listening to all of the negative, crybaby stuff. Yesterday I thought I was just being treated to more of the same when my one year old granddaughter, Audrey, was expressing her discomfort when we were eating breakfast in a restaurant. We had let her know several times that we didn't like to hear her whine and were about to take her out to the car for time out when we noticed that she was sitting on a fork. No one knows how the fork got in her high chair but removing it was all it took to improve Audrey's disposition. It caused me to wonder how many other people that I had gotten angry at during the last week for complaining had in fact also had a "fork in their chair." The phrase "fork in your chair" has come to mean that you have a real rather than a perceived grievance. Remembering the experience with Audrey helps to keep me from treating all complaints as being unworthy of giving credence. Some people and groups of people really do have a "fork in their chair." We need to listen to them and "remove the fork" if we have the power to do so.

Do It—A person should take all of the time that is needed to make a decision but the time that passes between the time that a decision is made and carrying it out is time wasted. Not only is the time wasted but it is also during this period of time that much mental and emotional stress builds up. Easing slowly into cold water may give the body the chance to slowly adjust to being uncomfortable but most of us would agree that it is best to jump right in and get it over with as quickly as possible. Suffering the short term pain of getting a tooth pulled is not fun, but it sure beats having a toothache for hours and even days. It's not the people that you fire that give you ulcers, but the ones you knew you should have fired but didn't. If you know you must do something that you hate to do, like suspend a kid and suffer the inevitable verbal abuse from the parents, it is best to JUST DO IT.

At-Risk Wood and At-Risk Kids—I have always liked the old saying, "One man's garbage is another man's treasure." I just love to search for treasures at auctions, animal shelters, and flea markets. It is satisfying to convert something that is considered trash or scrap into an item that is has some utilitarian value. In the same way, nothing is more exciting to an educator than to have some part in changing an at-risk student into a productive adult. Before we can start helping an at-risk student, or make something useful out of scrap wood, we must do two things: (1) we must be engaged with the material we are working with on an upclose and personal level, and (2) we must quit being mad at the material we hope to change and not consider it hopeless.

My former custodian and close friend recently had the outside of his house remodeled. He told me that he had some scrap wood that he wanted to get rid of and wondered if I wanted any of it to burn in my fireplace. It is well known by my friends that I take anything that is free. I told him to bring the wood over and put it on my patio. I had no idea how much wood he was talking about. Much to my surprise, when I came home from work, there was a huge pile of lumber on my patio that had been on the outside of my buddy's house. It took me about a week, working for several hours each evening, just to pull all of the old nails out of the lumber. I kind of got to know and appreciate the wood while pulling nails out of it and started to formulate some grand plans in my mind about things I could make out of it. The old positive thinking educator that I had become over the years, getting my kicks out of making something out of at-risk kids, now was taking the form of seeking satisfaction from changing this "scrap" wood that others thought was only fit to be burned, into something worthwhile. I made a picnic table that looks more like a huge meat chopping block than a table. It weighs so much that it takes four adults to move it. I also made enough heavy duty benches to last a lifetime.

Sure enough, those old scrap boards were still of some value. And I have never enjoyed anything more than spending my summer working with that valuable wood.

A Lifeguard Stand—located just outside of the bathhouse of the old Gage Park swimming pool during the early 1950s put me in an excellent position to observe how various persons solve problems. To get from the bathhouse to the swimming pool, a person was required to walk on a slab of concrete approximately 20 feet long. The concrete was in the direct sunlight and therefore, on a typical sunny July day, it would feel extremely hot on bare feet. I passed my time observing how various types of individuals reacted to the pain caused by the heat on the bottom of their feet. Reactions fell into three categories.

When the person got halfway across the section of hot concrete, he or she felt the pain and then:

(1) Just hurried on to the pool. The pain was then behind and the destination reached.

(2) Turned around and hurried back to the bathhouse. He was then back where he started from and the problem of how to cross the hot concrete remained. He now at least knew more about the problem and could look at various options and possible solutions. He felt no pain now from the heat but did feel anxiety and frustration because of what he now knew was ahead of him.

(3) Started jumping from one foot to the other crying loudly and doing nothing to solve the problem. He whined, moaned, and felt helpless, but the pain continued and he got no closer to his desired destination. Eventually someone else would come along and rescue him from his predicament. He never learned anything from his experience except to depend on others.

We have a choice to react to all of the difficulties, problems, and pains that we face in life in any one of the ways explained above. A "people watcher" can observe persons using all three methods every day. A conscious effort should be made to use method number one whenever possible. We need to get problems behind us, get to where we want to get, and move on. Occasionally we need to back off for some reason and reflect on solutions—use method number two. It is never productive to use method number three.

We need to do something. To just remain uncomfortable and whine is not an acceptable problem solving technique. People who do this get ulcers, are unhappy, and die an early death.

Thumbs Up Call Slips—I enjoy calling students who excel in some way into my office to visit with me. I send them a "Thumbs Up Call

Slip," which is a written sheet that invites the student to use it as a ticket to come to my office to visit informally with me. They can pick a time that is convenient for them to come and when both they and their teacher agree that missing class for a short time won't hurt their academic achievement. They know that they take the chance that I might not be able to see them at that time—in which case they go back to class and come back some other time. It is good for me to talk to successful students and it is a great way to re-inforce positive behavior. Most students like to come with another student or two, which is fine. Most of the time we just have a friendly visit but, over the years, many really neat ideas have had their origin in these sessions. I first met some present day adult friends in one of these "Thumbs Up" sessions when they were students. It's such a simple and inexpensive way to accomplish so much that I don't understand why more school administrators don't try it. Kids like it, parents like it, and it is great for the mental health of administrators.

To Keep Your Morale High—

(1)   Attend church services every Sunday; to keep your spirit in good shape.

(2)   Attend Optimist club once a week; to keep your attitude charged up.

(3)   Eat nutritious meals and exercise every day; to keep your body in good shape.

(4)   Back Notre Dame in football, even though you aren't Catholic. They usually win and then you feel like a winner.

(5   Check to make sure that your clothing still fits.

The human body is constantly changing. It is dynamic rather than static. It has a tendency to get larger as we age. If we aren't careful, our clothing will get out-dated or too small. This condition will make us very uncomfortable and hard to get along with.

In the same way, the field of education is constantly changing. It is also dynamic rather than static. Usually, expectations of us get larger as time goes by. We need to constantly check to make sure that the basic assumptions that fit in the past are not out-dated or in need of expansion. Our philosophy and ways of operating may need to be adjusted. If we don't do this, we can get very uncomfortable and hard to get along with.

I have found that the little "collar extender" that you can buy in clothing stores can make a size 17 shirt fit like a size 18. It is not only practical but it could also be seen as a symbol—that we need to enlarge or extend our understandings of the educational concepts that underlie our job so we can adjust to larger expectations and won't constantly feel strangled.

The Pendulum—We were complaining in our staff meeting about some of the trends that have recently been in vogue in the field of education. The comment was made, "Just wait a while and the pendulum will swing back the other way." Just passively and quietly wait! Are we only spectators in the game of life? As professionals, don't we have an obligation to cause things to happen in our field of expertise? We need to be advocates for causes in which we believe strongly. We need to be a social force. We must band together with others who believe as we do and form pressure groups. A pendulum begins to swing in one direction or the other because it is pushed in that direction. It continues to swing because of the force of gravity, a natural force. Social changes in direction happen because of social forces, not just because a certain amount of time has passed. We need to cause the social pendulum to swing—not just wait for it to happen. We need to get actively involved!

If The Superintendent Nods His Head, The School Could Be Sold—If you've ever attended an auction, you know that you must be careful at these functions when you nod your head, wink an eye, or raise an arm. You could end up owning some object that you never even considered buying because the auctioneer mistakenly translated your body language as a bid on the item. In the school environment everyone else can nod, sneeze, yell, or give input in any of a dozen ways, and no one pays much attention. But if the superintendent so much as nods his head, others begin assigning meaning to his actions. The Yes Men, who sit close to the superintendent, and the Nodders who are further down the line can yell "Yes" and nod and express opinions to their hearts content, but they go totally unnoticed. But if the superintendent so much as utters a sound or nods his head, it is like E.F. Hutton has spoken. All action ceases, all ears listen and those present utter, "What did he mean by that?"

Children Need To Experience Success—A farmer had a seven-year-old son and identical twin hunting dogs. He wanted to teach his son to hunt. He also wanted to train his identical twin dogs to retrieve birds out of the lake after they had been shot. The farmer decided that he would train one dog and let his son train the other one.

The farmer took his dog to the edge of the lake and, with his strong arm, threw a large stick out into the water. The stick went far out into the deep water. His dog attempted to fetch the stick but he soon got out into the turbulent and deep water and became tired, discouraged, and disillusioned. The dog returned to the edge of the lake without the stick. The farmer beat the dog with the stick and scolded him. The farmer continued for several months attempting to train the dog in the same manner. The dog became even less cooperative and never did learn to retrieve an object from the water.

The seven-year-old son was happy and excited about working with his pet dog. The two of them ran to the edge of the lake. The boy threw a small stick just barely into the water because his arm was not very strong.

The dog quickly stepped into the shallow water, picked up the small stick with his mouth, and brought it back to the boy. This act made both the dog and the boy very happy so they celebrated the success. As the months before hunting season passed the boy's arm grew stronger and he was able to throw a progressively larger stick further out into increasingly deep water. The dog responded by successfully retrieving these sticks and they both celebrated each success.

Hunting season opened and the dog the boy trained did a great job of retrieving birds and enjoyed every minute of the hunt. The dog the farmer trained didn't retrieve a single bird and had a miserable time. The farmer couldn't figure out why. "Must be something in the genes!", he muttered.

Parents who want their child to succeed in big tasks must provide opportunities for small successes early in life and celebrate each small success. A child will repeat those tasks that he succeeds at and gradually will have success at more advanced tasks. If a child is assigned too difficult a task at too early an age, he will become tired, discouraged, disillusioned, and uncooperative.

I'll Do It If I Can See That There Is Something In It For Me—
A city man and a country man agreed to enter their dogs in a race. The prize for the winning owner was an all expense paid trip to Las Vegas. Both men wanted to win so they immediately started training their dogs.

Every day the country man ran with his dog out to the wooded area of his farm. He sat on a log and thought beautiful thoughts while his dog enjoyed chasing rabbits and other wild creatures. The dog loved to run at top speed while chasing one rabbit and then stalk another rabbit until it became startled and then another chase would begin. When no rabbits could be found to chase, the man would throw a stick for the dog to run after and bring back to him. The man and his dog both enjoyed the routine so much that they did this every day and always stayed much longer in the woods than they had planned to.

The city man was the boss at a large corporation. He was accustomed to giving orders and having his subordinates execute his commands quickly. He would withhold their paychecks if they were slow to react and it was well known that he had fired several persons. He ordered one of his workers to take his dog to the company gymnasium and make it run. The employee succeeded in taking the dog to the gym but had no success at convincing him to run. The dog could see no reason to run and wasn't worried about the possibility of getting fired. The dog didn't even respond when advised that he could win a trip to Las Vegas for his owner. The dog was severely punished as a consequence of his disobedience but never did run.

The big race took place. The country man's dog won. The city man was heard commenting, "Next time I'll increase the punishment when my dog doesn't run. What that dog needs is more discipline." The city man didn't seem to understand that a dog will run because it wants to run, and sees a need to run, but it won't run because running may benefit his master.

No matter how much authority and power an adult perceives himself as having, he can't make children do something because he wants them to do it. Over an extended period, children (and all other persons for that matter) will only do those things that they want to do, feel a need to do, or see as being in their own best interest. Sometimes a person will do something just to please another person but only if pleasing the other person is something that he wants to do, feels a need to do, or sees as being in his own best interest.

We don't buy things from salesmen who give us "So I can win a prize" as the reason for us to buy something from them. We purchase things when we need them, not when someone else needs to sell them. The old statement "Do it because I told you to do it," will only work until the person who made the statement is out of sight.

Much more can be accomplished by creating a positive feeling tone and developing a good relationship with the learner than by attempting to use coercion, fear, and power.

Arts and Humanities—With some time off from work, I enjoyed listening to some of my favorite music. I have noticed that my appreciation for the Arts and Humanities has grown over the years. I can't pass up an opportunity to buy beautiful paintings at garage sales and auctions even though I know they will only end up on the wall in my own garage. When a person is young, there is the tendency to progress through life at a rapid pace and not take the time to "stop and smell the roses." To have a happy life a person must not only take the time to "smell the roses" but also hear the music, and to see beauty like clouds, rainbows, and sunsets. It is also very important to get to know, up-close and personal, the great artists who created great works. When we take the time to listen, we are surprised to discover that Great Composers really are great. Of course the greatest creator of beauty is God. One must thrive on being in the front row center instead of timidly existing in the back row. One must participate whenever possible by whistling along with the flutes when the band plays "Stars and Stripes Forever." The time and ability to concentrate and focus that is necessary to really enjoy great works of art becomes increasingly more available to a person with maturity. Early in life one tends to worry about acquiring the skills and knowledge that will make it possible to "make a living," and one forgets about those things that make life worth living. The means becomes the end rather than the means to an end. Job skills are tools to earn a living, but earning a living is not the same as living. Our goal should be to acquire skills and knowledge that will help us live a more fulfilled, enjoyable, and happy life. We should be more concerned about our quality of life than acquiring money. Schools must teach skills that students will need in the future to make a living; but it is even more important that we help students realize that there is more to life than making a living. They must have a reason to live. That is where the Arts and Humanities come in. Curriculum development specialists must understand the necessity of providing a strong music, art and humanities program, not as just a frill that a few can choose but as filling a basic need for all.

Harmony, Melody, and Cultural Diversity—Our Building Improvement Multi-cultural committee thought that we had discovered a great analogy to use to demonstrate the concept of cultural and racial harmony. We borrowed, from the music department, the idea that it takes four notes played at the same time to make good harmony. High pitched notes, low pitched notes, and those in between—each and every one contributes to create a pleasant sounding chord. Then we had a terrible thought! One of the notes, usually the highest one of the four, is considered to be the melody. Perhaps in our study of American History we have too often thought of the Caucasian race as the melody and others as having only a supporting role. When I sing bass in church, I don't get mad because the soprano gets to sing the melody, but I can understand why African Americans, and other minority groups, would not appreciate American History being taught as if Caucasian history was the melody. Or worse yet, to live their entire lives as if someone else, because of his skin color, got to sing the melody.

Retirement—I worked for 34 years within one block of Lyman Road, in North Topeka. I developed a love affair with that community. When the students heard that I was retiring, some of them worked with the staff and got permission from the Board of Education to name the school gymnasium in my honor. They surprised me by doing this at an all-school assembly. Later, a gala reception was held in my honor at the school, complete with tear-jerking speeches by several of my friends and co-workers. I was deeply moved and almost speechless.

The day finally arrived when my retirement became a reality rather than a general concept. The students and staff had all left for the summer and the building was empty. I cleaned out my office and gently placed items that I had accumulated over the years in a box. Each thing I picked up seemed to resist leaving and had a story to tell. I wanted to stay and reminisce, but time was passing. I hadn't expected bands to be playing and crowds to be cheering, but walking to my car alone, carrying all of my possessions in one cardboard box, had a somber finality about it that is hard to explain. It was a little bit like dying in that no matter how many people attend the funeral, a person must take the final act of leaving all alone. The difference is that when you die you don't even get to take a box full of stuff with you. It was beyond my comprehension that I would now simply walk out of the front door of the school, never to walk back in again as principal.

I have noticed that my life could be divided into four types of "times." First, were the days when I went to work; the teachers and kids were there, and I was definitely in the frying pan. Secondly, were the Sunday type days. Sundays have always been really special because that is the time that I feel closest to God at church and to my family at home. Our entire family gathers every Sunday after church to eat Grandma Myra's cooking together. Sunday evenings were just a little hard to enjoy because I knew, from painful experience, that Monday morning was not far off. I was not at work but I wasn't far from it. Thinking about Monday was worse than experiencing it. The third type of time, Saturday time, was when I usually had no commitments at school and could do what I wanted to do. The fourth type of time, the wonderful month of July was the best time of all.

When a patron asked me when I'm off for the summer I would reply, "That's like asking me when I'm not a grandpa." Being a principal of a school is not a job so much as an identity. It is like being a parent. You are never really "off," but sometimes you are more "on" than at other times. It is a 24 hour a day, 365 day a year job. A principal can hire a "baby-sitter" (the building and grounds staff) to care for the building in his absence, but the real body of the school (the staff, students, and patrons) demands his fulltime attention. No one else can take his place. So while I really was never "off" for the summer in the past, my responsibilities did change to a much less stress producing pace.

Well, I'm fully retired now. During the last several months before I retired, I marked off the days on a calendar in the garage. I'm leaving that calendar set on July. I'm going to live the rest of my life like it is July. Every week will be made up of six Saturdays followed by a Sunday. I'm planning on getting out of bed every day at about 8:00 a.m. instead of at 6:00 a.m. sharp. I can now exercise the ultimate rollover option which says that when I wake up in the morning I have the option of rolling over and going back to sleep. No more blue Sunday nights thinking about how bad it will be to get up the next morning. No more blue Mondays when I will have to work out all of the problems that kids got into over the weekend. No more trying to fool myself by setting all of my clocks seven minutes early so I will get where I must be early. No more being specific when I talk about time. Now I can talk like other people who add the suffix "ish" to time. I have always been surrounded by clocks. I have one in every room and on my wrist. I even rely on clocks to tell me when I am hungry. Punctuality is almost a part of my religion. I'm no longer a foot soldier in the trenches in the war against those foreign cultures who don't care what time it is. As the old saying goes, "If you can't beat them, join them."

From now on I won't be responsible for the actions of hundreds of other people, only my own. No more hating to hear the telephone ring. I can enjoy going to athletic contests and watch the game instead of the crowd.

More than anything else I'll miss the daily contact with my best friends both young and old. I've always needed people. I'm a people man. Actually experiencing retirement takes some of the humor out of the saying, "Old principals never die. They just lose their faculties." It is as if somebody else is sleeping in my bed and my educational family has a new dad. I will need to get a new identity. I have gone from serving proudly as captain of the team, ball carrier, and active participant on the field of life to passive observer of the actions of others and spectator in the stands. All of my career I have championed the cause of empowering staff members and giving them a feeling of being in control. Now I have no power and I am not in control of anything. As principal I always had an audience. Now I get the feeling that nobody out there is listening. I feel a loss of power, purpose, and identity. As principal I always felt that what I did made a difference in the lives of a large number of people. I am no longer of any use to anyone. I feel like the scrap wood that is replaced by new siding. I'm like an antique car that is blocked up in a museum, not going anywhere. I've always served; now I'm in a position of being served, and I'm not used to it. When race horses slow down, they are put out to stud. No guy in his right mind would complain about being put out to stud, but we all know that the next stop will most likely be the glue factory. I'm not sure that a person who has spent 38 years overcoming adversity and solving problems will be happy in a totally stress free environment. It will be like culture shock. Resting may not be as satisfying if I have nothing to rest up from. Maybe it takes weekdays to enjoy weekends and cold days in December to appreciate the warm days in July. Too many naps in the afternoon may cause me to not sleep well at night. How will I know when I am on vacation?

I'm in the dessert stage of life. I've eaten the main course (career and raising a family). It is time to enjoy the luxury of choice and sweetness and to enjoy the fruits of my labor. I've completed the required courses of life and can now enroll in electives that I choose and enjoy.

It is amazing how smart I have suddenly become. It is much easier to tell others what they ought to do than to have the responsibility of actually getting something done and suffering the consequences if it doesn't work.

Over the years I have observed many bandwagons pass by the education scene and have enthusiastically jumped on most of them myself. Anyone who didn't was "outdated, closed-minded, and old fashioned." These bandwagons all seemed to be headed in the right direction when we jumped on them, and we learned some valuable lessons from each of them. We thought that the latest bandwagon had all of the answers and would lead us to the one great way to organize education and teach. Time after time we were let down. Some in our profession soon became disillusioned and preferred to just be left alone and continue doing what they had done in the past. Becoming cynical and stagnant is an even worse mistake than jumping on bandwagons. Persons who make their living by educating others surely must believe in improving themselves through education. Riding on a bandwagon is like riding on a school bus; the person driving takes you, and everyone else on board, where he wants to take you. Educators need to get off of bandwagons and do the driving themselves. They need to keep moving and, by doing the driving themselves, they can choose where they are headed and how fast they proceed. This process depends on those who practice it to be eclectic—that is, to choose what appears to be the best from diverse sources, systems, or styles. We need to do our educational shopping from a large department store type environment rather than speciality shops with only one point of view. Teachers need to utilize an expert-to-expert improvement approach; recognizing that teachers are themselves experts at what they do. They should recognize that they began developing their teaching style, which has served them well, on the first day that they started student teaching. That style should be fine-tuned each day that they teach. They should keep those teaching behaviors that are productive and search to find alternative ways to teach those lessons that have been less successful. They should look to a variety of sources for help in constantly and continually improving. Most of the time when teaching behaviors are discarded and replaced it is as a result of routine, regular house keeping that occurs when we evaluate how our day went. Sometimes more radical change is desired and a "spring housecleaning" type process is called for. This process involves being willing to throw away some approaches that can be replaced with something new. Spring housecleaning at home is usually done only once a year when ample time is available. The same is generally true of making major changes in teaching style. Just as an accomplished gymnast makes few changes and works on his fine points, the experienced teacher usually doesn't find it necessary to make radical changes in teaching methods but works on details to make the good change to excellent.

A simple truth, that is far too often overlooked, is that nobody knows more about how to teach than the classroom teachers in elementary and secondary schools who meet face-to-face with real kids everyday. Teachers are experts, professionals, and the real unsung heros of America. I salute you!